Also by Marion Cunningham

The Supper Book
The Fannie Farmer Cookbook (thirteenth edition)
The Fannie Farmer Baking Book
The Breakfast Book
The Fannie Farmer Cookbook (twelfth edition)

COOKING WITH
CHILDREN

with illustrations by Emily Lisker
and photographs by Penina Meisels

MARION CUNNINGHAM

COOKING WITH CHILDREN

Fifteen lessons for children, age 7 and up,
who really want to learn to cook

Alfred A. Knopf   New York   1996

This Is a Borzoi Book
Published by Alfred A. Knopf, Inc.

Library of Congress Cataloging-in-Publication Data
Cunningham, Marion.
Cooking with children: Fifteen lessons for children, age 7 and up, who
really want to learn to cook   /   by Marion Cunningham. —1st ed.
p.   cm.
Includes index
ISBN 0-679-42297-8
1. Cookery—Juvenile literature.   [1. Cookery.]   I. Title.
TX652.5.C86   1995
641.5'123—dc20   95-13580
CIP
AC

Manufactured in the United States of America
Published November 9, 1995
Reprinted Once
Third printing, June 1996

To Evan and Judith Jones

Acknowledgments

Special gratitude to my young missionaries, Sara and Katie Connett, and their mother, Patti Connett, for joining in this adventure of learning to be home cooks; and to all the enthusiastic children in my classes, who shared with me their lively curiosity, high spirits, and awakening talents. And a loud thank you to Fritz Streiff, for rallying to the completion of this book with good humor and talent; to Barbara Walker, for sharing her inspiration and common sense, and for her classic, *The Little House Cookbook*; and to all my friends for helping in every way they could, especially Michael Bauer, Meg Collins, Jan Cooper, Bill Jayme, Jane Moore, Nancy Schroeder, Comfort Scott, Helen Mary Stein, and Catherine Cunningham, my daughter, who also helped with the children's classes at both the recreation center and at home.

I want to give an extra thank-you to the following children who spent time beyond our lessons helping me find safer or simpler ways to prepare and cook some of our recipes: Jessica Clark, Nico Jones, Oliver Jones, Kate-Marie Russell, Olivia Russell, Elizabeth Zedaker, and Peter Zedaker.

And thank you to all the children who served as models for both the line art and the photographs: Ansarys Andino, Sebastian Dumonet, Vanessa Dumonet, Kris Carlow, Jordan Connett, David Ecker, Allie Halperin, Jim Hess, Laura Hess, Dana Johnson, Lisa Johnson, Julisa LeBron, Brendan McClenahan, Connor McClenahan, Linda Nguyen, and Bethany Santana.

Contents

Why This Book?

I have written this book because I feel strongly that cooking and eating together is a satisfaction that is rapidly disappearing from our lives. Working away from home has become a necessity for most adults, and kitchens are no longer the center of home life. We still nourish ourselves, but we have let something far more important slip away. Enjoying food together is a way of connecting with one another, and we are losing those values we unconsciously learned and absorbed day after day as we shared meals together and exchanged conversation.

Teaching children how to cook, I think, is our greatest hope for recapturing what we have lost. The earlier you can get the feel of the kitchen the easier it is to become a good home cook. Two years ago, I began teaching children's classes. I first taught classes of twelve children, age seven through eleven, at our community center. My purpose was to discover what they could or couldn't do physically when learning the basics of cooking. They often looked awkward or clumsy stirring or chopping, but they caught on quickly and always achieved decent results. They were clearly impressed by the transformation of raw ingredients into surprisingly good food, and most of them chose to take home what they had cooked to share with their families. I could tell that they felt both pleasure and pride in their accomplishment.

For the last year I have been teaching only one or two children at a time, in my home, so I could learn what they really thought about the different aspects of cooking, what they liked and what they didn't like, what was easy and what was hard to do. The fifteen basic lessons in this book are based on my observations and the conversations we had during these classes. My assumption is that an adult will be around to supervise the children as they use this book, but I have been careful to give detailed enough directions so that youngsters from about seven and up can follow them on their own. In each lesson the children learn new techniques, which are then put into practice again and again as they move on to more demanding challenges. I have kept ingredients to a minimum. No electrical equipment is used, because touching, smelling, and seeing the ingredients and the ways they change as they're being prepared and cooked teach far more than you might realize—and preparing food this way is safer.

The lessons I've learned from teaching children to cook are: Don't try to make finished cooks out of beginning cooks. Don't give alternate steps unless absolutely necessary. Don't give substitutions for ingredients. Keep the cooking simple.

Giving these classes has been a great experience. It has been a revelation to me how capable and curious children can be in the kitchen, and how interested and intrigued they are by simple home cooking. And in translating all I have learned onto these pages I hope to give the children using this book and the parent or other grown-up working with them all the confidence—as well as all the basic tools—they need, so that when they have mastered the fifteen lessons they can cook just about anything.

Since I've become a missionary on this subject of cooking at home—and more important, on eating together—I hope I will convert a few of the children into becoming missionaries too. And it will be a bonus if some of the youngsters find the same lifelong, constant pleasure in cooking and baking that I have found.

A Word
to Young Cooks

Why should you want to learn to cook? Because cooking can bring so many wonderful experiences into your life!

There is mystery in cooking; no matter how many times you make the same dish, it will never be exactly the same. Think how remarkable it is that you can take some flour, butter, sugar, and an egg and turn these into cookies; or that you can simply stir two eggs together and gently cook them into creamy scrambled eggs.

You will learn something about chemistry when you see the effects of mixing different ingredients together, and something about mathematics when you figure out fractions. Maybe most important of all, you will learn something about patience when you make something and it doesn't turn out, and you have to make it all over again.

When you feel a little troubled, there is nothing that can absorb your attention and lift your spirits like going into the kitchen, washing your hands, and starting to cook or bake. And there is nothing like the deep sense of accomplishment you will feel when you share the food you've cooked with your family and friends.

As you grow older and learn more about cooking, you will find friends who like to cook too, and it is fun to swap recipes and cook together. Cooking begins at home, but it can take you all over the world, discovering what people like to eat in places like China, Japan, Italy, and France. When you learn to cook, you will want to travel and taste the dishes you've read about. You can follow your fork around the world, meeting new friends and sharing the excitement of cooking.

A Word to Adults About Safety

When you do these lessons with children, you need to watch carefully that they do not cut themselves or burn themselves as they remove a dish from a hot oven or lift the lid off a boiling pot. Younger children may need supervision for some of these tasks. When a knife is required in a lesson, I have found that some of the youngest children are more secure using an 8-inch serrated knife rather than a paring knife (see page 9). Older children can be introduced to a chopping (or "chef's") knife (see page 85).

It is important to advise children always to be careful when handling knives and when using heat, but too much repeated concern can make them timid.

THE RIGHT HEIGHT

It is important when you are cutting, slicing, chopping, and mixing ingredients or kneading dough to have your work surface the right height. The average kitchen countertop is too high for most of you, so either find a work table about 6 inches lower than the counter or else get a stool and stand on it. Your work surface should come to your waist so you have the full strength of your arms and hands to chop vegetables, roll out dough, and knead bread. The table illustrated here and throughout these pages was just the right height for the children who were making these recipes. When they were working at the stove, most of them stood on a small stool.

A FRIENDLY BOWL OF WARM WATER

The best friend you will have in the kitchen is a big bowl of warm, soapy water, waiting to soak all the kitchen tools and dishes and pans that you use. If you dump your dirty things in right away, they'll be so much easier to clean. If you leave them lying around so the food on them gets dry, you have to work much harder to get them clean. If you clean up while you are waiting for water to boil, or for something to cool or bake, you will never mind doing all the clean-up when you finish cooking.

COOKING WITH
CHILDREN

Chapter 1

VEGETABLE SOUP

WHAT YOU LEARN MAKING

VEGETABLE SOUP

1. HOW TO PEEL AND CHOP VEGETABLES.

2. HOW TO SAUTÉ ONIONS, CARROTS, AND CELERY TO BRING OUT THEIR FLAVORS. TO "SAUTÉ" MEANS TO STIR SOMETHING IN A LITTLE BUTTER OR OIL (YOU'LL LEARN MORE ABOUT SAUTÉING IN CHAPTER 8, PAGE 78).

3. WHAT "BOILING" AND "SIMMERING" MEAN.

4. HOW TO BE ORGANIZED—ONE OF THE MOST IMPORTANT LESSONS IN COOKING! FOR THIS RECIPE, IT MEANS PUTTING THE INGREDIENTS OUT ON THE COUNTER AND PREPARING THEM BEFORE YOU BEGIN TO COOK. ALWAYS READ THE RECIPE BEFOREHAND AND HAVE EVERYTHING LINED UP SO YOU'RE NOT FRANTICALLY TRYING TO CHOP THE TOMATO WHEN IT'S TIME TO ADD IT TO THE SOUP.

Soup is a wonderful
dish to make. It is
warm and comfort-
ing on a chilly day
and you really feel
you have cooked
something special
for yourself and others
when you put down on the table bowls filled with vegetables in good broth. Try toasting a few slices of French
bread, put the butter nearby, and you will have a foolproof
meal that everyone can enjoy.

The vegetable soup you make in this first lesson is halfway between a light soup and a filling one. Here are the great facts about
soup: You can always make it more filling and you can always make
it feed more people. Just add cooked rice, potatoes, or pasta, and
more water or broth, if the soup needs it. A generous serving for
each person is about one and a half cups of soup.

VEGETABLE SOUP

Don't buy giant-sized vegetables when you make this soup. The smaller ones are younger and have lots more flavor and tenderness.

EQUIPMENT LIST

PARING KNIFE OR 8-INCH SERRATED KNIFE

CUTTING BOARD

2 SMALL BOWLS

VEGETABLE PEELER

2 1/2-QUART SAUCEPAN

1 CUP MEASURING CUP

LARGE WOODEN SPOON

SOUP LADLE

4 SOUP BOWLS

1 ONION

1 CARROT

1 STALK CELERY

1 TOMATO

1 ZUCCHINI

2 TABLESPOONS BUTTER

SALT AND PEPPER

4 CUPS CHICKEN BROTH, CANNED OR HOMEMADE

PREPARING THE ONION:

1. Use a paring knife to trim off the fuzzy small brown root end and the tan papery top of the onion and discard them. With the paring knife make a cut into the papery outer skin of the onion, then peel it all off with your fingers and throw it away. Cut the onion in half from stem top to root end. Put the onion halves cut side down on a

4

cutting board. Cut 8 or 9 slices crosswise from each half, about the thickness of 2 pennies. As you slice, curl under the ends of the fingers of your hand holding the onion so that you don't cut your fingertips with the knife; move your hand back on the onion after each slice. Cut the slices into 3 equal parts. Scoop all the onion pieces into a small bowl and set the bowl near the stove.

PREPARING THE CARROT:

2. Slice off the coarse top and the bottom tip of the carrot with a paring knife and discard. Holding the thick top of the carrot in one hand and the vegetable peeler in your other hand slide the peeler down the length of the carrot, pressing just hard enough to remove the coarse peel. Keep turning the carrot slightly and repeat the motion from top to bottom until you have removed all the peel.

Put the carrot on a cutting board and cut the carrot in half lengthwise. Put each half flat side down and cut crosswise into half-moon slices the same thickness as the onion slices. Add the carrot slices to the onion in the bowl near the stove.

PREPARING THE CELERY:

3. Wash the celery stalk and dry it. Place it rounded side up on the cutting board. Slice it crosswise into half-moon pieces the same thickness as the carrot and onion slices, and add them to the same bowl with the other vegetables near the stove.

PREPARING THE TOMATO:

4. With the tip of a paring knife, cut out the little round brown stem top of the tomato by cutting around it. Discard it. Now cut the tomato in half from stem top to bottom. Put the halves on a cutting board, cut side down. Cut each tomato half crosswise into 6 or 8 slices, just as you did with the onion. Cut the slices into 3 pieces. Put them into a separate bowl and set aside.

PREPARING THE ZUCCHINI:

5. Zucchini does not need to be peeled—the bright green skin is tender and pleasant to eat. Just rinse off the zucchini and dry it. Remove the hard stem end and the tip. Now cut the zucchini in half lengthwise, the same way you cut the carrot. Put the flat sides down on your cutting board and cut half-moon slices the thickness of 2 pennies, the same size as the carrot slices. Put the zucchini slices into the bowl with the tomato and place the bowl near the stove so that it's right at hand when time to add these vegetables to the soup.

VARIATIONS

If you want to make this vegetable soup thicker and more filling, and to have extra servings, add 2 cups cooked rice, or 2 cups cooked diced potatoes cut the size of small dice, or 2 cups small cooked pasta, such as small macaroni, at the same time you add the zucchini and tomato.

PUTTING IT ALL TOGETHER:

6. Put a 2 1/2-quart saucepan on the stove and turn the heat to medium-high. Put the 2 tablespoons butter into the saucepan, and as the butter melts, tilt the saucepan a little, up and down and around, so the butter covers the bottom of the pan. Now turn the heat down to medium low.

7. Add the onions, carrots, and celery, stirring to mix and coat them with butter. Cook, stirring the vegetables often, for 5 minutes. Shake a little salt and pepper over the vegetables and stir them again.

8. Pour the 4 cups chicken broth into the saucepan and stir so the vegetables are well mixed with the broth. Turn the heat up to medium-high so the broth begins to boil. (Liquid is at a boil when it is bubbling busily all over the surface and giving off steam.) As soon as the broth boils, turn the heat to low so the broth will simmer. (Liquid is simmering when there are just a few bubbles forming on top of the broth.) Simmer for 5 minutes. Add the tomatoes and zucchini and cook the soup for 3 or 4 more minutes. Now dip a large spoon into the soup and cool the broth a little by blowing on it. Taste it, and if it doesn't have much flavor, salt it lightly, and taste it again. You have to be the judge of your own cooking. Remember, you're the cook and you're in charge! As you learn to taste critically, you will be surprised at how many times just adding a little more salt or pepper can make your dish a lot better.

HOW TO MEASURE A SAUCEPAN

To choose the right size saucepan, measure how much liquid it holds. For example, to make sure you have a 2 1/2-quart saucepan for this recipe, fill a 2-cup measuring cup with water and pour it into a saucepan you think is about the right size. (You can use a saucepan that is a little larger, but not any smaller.) Fill the 2-cup measuring cup five times and keep pouring the water into the pan. (Each time you fill the measuring cup with two cups, you get one pint, or half a quart.) If the pan holds all the water, right to the top, it is a 2 1/2-quart saucepan.

9. Put the soup bowls near the stove and use a soup ladle to dip the soup out of the pot into each bowl. (A soup ladle is a large deep-rounded spoon on a long handle.) Without getting too fussy about it, try to dish up about the same amount of broth and vegetables for each soup bowl. Vegetable soup should be served hot.

LEARNING TO USE YOUR STOVE

Most stoves today use either electric or gas heat and they have clearly marked dials or handles that tell you how to set the degree of heat you need. All you have to do is turn the dial to the left and stop at the number on the dial for the amount of heat you need.

I have an electric stove and this is what one of my dials looks like and what the numbers mean:

1 and 2: low heat for barely simmering

3: medium-to-low heat for simmering with more bubbles

4 and 5: medium heat for gentle boiling

6: hot for boiling and sautéing

7 and HI: very hot for fast boiling and frying

The important difference between gas and electric heat is that with gas heat you can instantly turn the heat on, instantly change it, and instantly turn it off. You can also see whether the flame is high, medium, or low.

Electric heat has electric coils instead of a gas flame so it takes a few seconds for the coil to get heated, a few seconds to change the heat, and a few seconds for the coil to cool down. As a result, when you are cooking and you want to lower the heat immediately (because maybe your onions are starting to burn), you must slide your pan or skillet off the burner, turn the heat lower, and let the electric coil cool down for one minute; then return the pan or skillet to the stove.

TOOLS FOR PEELING, CUTTING, SLICING, AND CHOPPING

A vegetable peeler is the best tool for peeling many vegetables and fruits. It not only does a good job, but also is very safe to use when you are first learning the "tricks of the trade."

Another good beginning tool is an 8-inch serrated knife. The word "serrated" means that the blade has lots of small grooves along the edge. These grooves dig into whatever you are cutting, or slicing, so the blade doesn't slip as easily as a regular knife. After you've used a serrated knife for a while, you will feel secure using a regular paring knife.

You'll be surprised at how attached you can become to a favorite knife or tool. When children come to my house for a cooking lesson, I spread a few different knives out on a table so they can pick each one up and feel the differences. Some knives and tools fit their hands better than others and they know right away what suits them best.

Chapter 2

SALADS SMALL and LARGE

WHAT YOU LEARN MAKING

THESE SALADS

1. HOW TO TASTE CRITICALLY AND CORRECT THE BALANCE IN A SIMPLE SALAD DRESSING.

2. HOW TO PREPARE SALAD GREENS.

3. HOW TO HARD-BOIL EGGS AND HOW TO MIX A TASTY MAIN-COURSE SALAD.

Salads are popu-
lar with most
people, and even
with cats and dogs, as you
know if you've ever watched them out-
doors chewing green grass. And we all know how contented cows
are grazing on grass all day long.

Small green salads are often part of lunch or dinner, and we
like them because they are cold and raw, which makes a happy
contrast to hot, cooked dishes.

A large salad can be the main event in a meal. If there are a few
cans of tuna on the shelf, tuna salad is always an easy answer to the
question, "What shall we have to eat?" And leftover tuna salad
makes a great sandwich. A big salad is also a perfect way to make
use of leftover cooked chicken, turkey, or ham.

OIL AND VINEGAR DRESSING
(Vinaigrette)

A salad dressing must be balanced, like a good glass of lemonade. When you make lemonade you need just the right amount of sugar to tame the sourness of the lemon. With salad dressing you need enough oil to tame the sourness of vinegar.

EQUIPMENT LIST

MEASURING SPOONS

SMALL BOWL

TEASPOON

1 TABLESPOON CIDER VINEGAR

1 TABLESPOON COLD WATER

1/4 TEASPOON SALT

4 TABLESPOONS OLIVE OIL

1. Put the tablespoon of vinegar, cold water, and 1/4 teaspoon salt into a small bowl. Stir the mixture with a spoon for a few seconds, then let it sit for 1 minute, so the salt dissolves.

2. Pour in the 4 tablespoons olive oil and stir, holding the edge of the bowl with one hand and your spoon in the other.

Keep your eye on the dressing and you will see a change in the way it looks. It will become thick, yellow, and cloudy instead of thin and clear. That is the way you want your dressing to look when you add it to the salad. Now taste the dressing by dipping a lettuce leaf into it and pop the coated leaf into your mouth. If it tastes good, it's ready to go, but if you feel it needs a little more salt, vinegar, or oil, add just a little of what it seems to need and taste it again. Tasting is important. The dressing won't remain blended for more than a minute or two, so when it is time to use the dressing, be sure to stir it again before you add it to the salad.

GREEN SALAD

SERVES 3 (MAKES ABOUT 6 CUPS)

1 LARGE HEAD OF ROMAINE; OR 2 SMALL HEADS OF

OAKLEAF, RED LEAF, OR BUTTER LETTUCE

1/3 CUP VINAIGRETTE (SEE PRECEDING RECIPE,

PAGE 12)

EQUIPMENT LIST

PARING KNIFE OR 8-INCH
SERRATED KNIFE

COLANDER

SALAD BOWL

1. Choose any green lettuces you like. You don't have to measure the exact quantity of lettuce leaves, but in case you're wondering, this much lettuce makes about 6 cups when the leaves are washed, dried, and torn into bite-sized pieces— enough to make a nice serving for three people. Tear off and throw away any coarse, wilted outer leaves. Cut off the stem end of the lettuces and separate the leaves.

2. Wash the leaves in the sink by putting them in a colander under cold, running water and tossing the leaves gently, allowing the water to run all over them. After about a minute, turn off the water and shake the colander so most of the water drains off. Now tear the leaves into bite-sized pieces and pat them dry with paper towels. It is important to dry the leaves

so that the salad dressing will stick to them; otherwise the dressing runs off the leaves and makes a puddle in the bottom of the salad bowl. You can wash the lettuces in advance and keep them in the refrigerator wrapped in a paper towel in a plastic bag until you're ready to make the salad.

3. Put the washed and dried leaves in a salad bowl. Stir the dressing again to blend it, then drizzle it over the greens. Use your clean hands to toss gently, turning and reaching into the bottom of the bowl so that all the leaves get coated with the dressing. Serve the salad as soon as you have added the dressing, because that's when it is best. If the leaves sit around in the dressing, they will get soggy.

TUNA SALAD

SERVES 3 (MAKES 5 1/2 CUPS)

2 EGGS

ONE 6-OUNCE CAN TUNA (1/2 CUP)

2 STALKS CELERY

1/2 HEAD ICEBERG LETTUCE

5 TABLESPOONS MAYONNAISE (ABOUT 1/3 CUP)

3 TABLESPOONS SWEET PICKLE RELISH

1 TEASPOON LEMON JUICE

SALT AND PEPPER

EQUIPMENT LIST

SMALL SAUCEPAN

KITCHEN TIMER

LARGE SPOON

SMALL- AND MEDIUM-SIZED
   BOWLS

CAN OPENER

FORK

PARING KNIFE OR 8-INCH
   SERRATED KNIFE

CUTTING BOARD

SALAD BOWL

MEASURING SPOONS

3 PLATES

1. Put the 2 eggs into a small saucepan and cover them with water. Put the pan on a stove burner and turn the heat on to medium-high. Set the kitchen timer for 5 minutes. When the bell rings, turn the heat down to medium and set the timer again for 10 minutes. When the timer rings, turn the heat off and slide the pan off the burner. Use a large spoon to fish one egg at a time out of the pan and put it into a small bowl of cold water.

2. Open the can of tuna but leave the lid in place. Take the can to the sink, and press the lid firmly against the tuna, turning the can upside down so the liquid in the can drains out. Press

Preparing salad greens and tasting critically the vinaigrette by dipping a lettuce leaf into the dressing

Breakfast in the garden with omelets, pancakes, and popovers

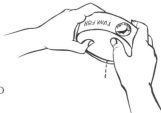

hard; there is more liquid than you think. Remove the lid and throw it away. Remove the tuna from the can with a fork and put it into a medium-sized bowl. If the tuna is in chunks, break it into small pieces with your fork or your fingers. Set aside.

3. Wash the 2 celery stalks and cut away the coarse uneven bottom and top. Cut or break the stalks in half lengthwise. Put the halves on a cutting board round side down and cut them lengthwise into 3 long strips with a paring knife. Line the pieces up together. While holding the

pieces together with one hand, cut pieces crosswise about the thickness of 2 pennies. As you slice, curl the ends of your fingers under so that you don't cut your fingertips when the knife gets close. Put the celery pieces into the bowl with the tuna.

4. You need only half a head of iceberg lettuce for this tuna salad. If you are starting with a whole head, take a paring knife and with the point cut a deep circle around the thick core. Pry the core out and discard it. Remove any tired-looking old leaves from the head of lettuce and throw them away. Hold the head in the sink under cold running water, with the hole where you pried out the core right under the tap. Let the water run into the leaves for 2 or 3 seconds. Now turn the head upside down and shake it so all the water runs out. This freshens the leaves.

Cut the head in half from top to bottom. Put one half of the head of lettuce in a plastic bag and place it in the refrigerator. Put the other half on a cutting board, flat side down. Start slicing downward, crosswise to the original cut, cutting the lettuce into slices about the thickness of a slice of bread. The slices usually fall over on their sides. Leave them in a stack where they fall. When you have sliced all the lettuce, turn the slices around and cut them into 4 pieces. Use your fingers to separate the leaves so you have lots of small pieces of lettuce. Put them in a salad bowl.

5. Take the eggs out of the water. Crack the shells on the hard edge of the counter or on the edge of a bowl. Use your fingers to peel off the shells and the skin underneath. It is hard to see this skin but you can feel it. When both eggs are peeled, cut them in half lengthwise, and then cut the halves in two lengthwise. Now cut crosswise so you have small pieces of egg white and yolk. Add the chopped eggs to the salad bowl.

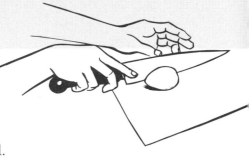

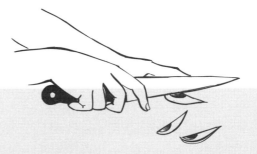

6. Sprinkle the tuna and celery over the eggs.

7. Now it's time to make the dressing for the salad. Measure the 1/3 cup of mayonnaise into a small bowl. Measure the 3 tablespoons of sweet pickle relish and stir it into the mayonnaise. Cut 1 lemon in half crosswise. Poke a fork into the middle of the cut side of a lemon half. Holding the lemon in one hand and the fork in the other, squeeze the lemon juice into a little cup or bowl, by twisting the lemon and turning it so the juice runs into the cup or bowl. You need only 1 teaspoon, so stop when you think you have enough. Remove any seeds. Add the teaspoon of lemon juice to the 1/3 cup of mayonnaise and stir again to mix everything together.

With a teaspoon, scoop up a little of the mayonnaise and taste it to see whether it needs a little more pickle relish or lemon juice or whether it is fine just as it is. If you like the dressing, add it to the tuna salad. Spoon the dressing on top of the salad and lightly stir and toss so the dressing is spread evenly over the tuna, celery, eggs, and lettuce. Now taste and add a little salt and pepper if you think it needs more seasoning. If you are ready to eat, divide the salad onto the 3 plates, sit down, spread your napkin on your lap, and enjoy the best moment of all, time to eat.

If you are going to eat later, cover the bowl with plastic wrap and refrigerate the salad until it is time to eat. Any leftover tuna salad will make a good sandwich for tomorrow's lunch.

> ### VARIATIONS
> This salad is delicious made with leftover chicken, turkey, or ham. Just use 1/2 to 1 cup of chopped cooked chicken, turkey, or ham (or a combination) instead of the 1/2 cup of tuna called for in the recipe.

Chapter 3

HAMBURGERS
and MEATLOAF

WHAT YOU LEARN MAKING

HAMBURGERS and MEATLOAF

1. THE SECRET OF WHAT KEEPS A HAMBURGER MOIST AND TENDER.

2. HOW TO HANDLE THE MEAT AND HOW TO MIX AND FORM PATTIES OR A LOAF.

3. HOW TO TEST THE HEAT OF YOUR SKILLET.

4. HOW TO PAN-FRY.

5. HOW TO TEST FOR DONENESS.

6. HOW TO BAKE AND SERVE A MEATLOAF.

If we all got to vote on our favorite food, I'll bet hamburgers would be the number one winner. When you make hamburgers, there are some rules to follow so you will make a winner too. You need to use fresh ground beef, crisp lettuce, and a soft bun. Most important is to learn how to make a moist

hamburger patty. The secret is in the way you handle the meat, so read your recipe carefully.

Meatloaf is an old-fashioned dish that many of us still make and enjoy. I loved it when I was a child and I still make it today. We used to have meatloaf every Wednesday night when I was growing up. In fact, everyone in our neighborhood in a small town in southern California had meatloaf every Wednesday. And many of us thought it was better than the roast beef we all had on Sunday. It was the same way in most of America then, and it was comforting to know just what you were going to have for dinner.

Meatloaf and hamburger are cousins. Both are made with ground beef and are usually flavored with onions and tomato sauce or ketchup, but meatloaf has breadcrumbs and an egg added to the mixture so it holds together when cooked and can be sliced. A hamburger sits in your hand and is fun to eat; meatloaf sits on your plate with dignity, and you eat it with a fork. They are both delicious. And leftover meatloaf has a bonus for you because it makes a great sandwich the next day.

HAMBURGERS

The most important point to remember in order to make a juicy, moist hamburger or meatloaf is to handle the meat gently and lightly while you are mixing and forming it. If you squeeze and press the meat roughly you will have dry, tough, firm meat when it is cooked. This seems to be a secret that most people don't know, and it will make your home-cooked hamburgers so much better than all the take-out hamburgers.

1 POUND GROUND BEEF

1/2 TEASPOON SALT

1/4 TEASPOON PEPPER

1/4 CUP WATER

CONDIMENTS:

    MUSTARD

    MAYONNAISE

    TOMATO KETCHUP

    ONION SLICES

    TOMATO SLICES

    CHEESE SLICES

    PICKLES

    ICEBERG LETTUCE

EQUIPMENT LIST

MIXING BOWL

MEASURING SPOONS

MEASURING CUPS

LARGE SKILLET

METAL SPATULA

PARING KNIFE

1 TABLESPOON VEGETABLE OIL

4 HAMBURGER BUNS

1. Put the ground beef in a mixing bowl. Sprinkle the 1/2 teaspoon salt and 1/4 teaspoon pepper over the meat and add the 1/4 cup water, and gently mix them into the meat with your hands. Remember, don't handle the meat any more than you have to, and above all, don't squeeze it; just mix it lightly with your fingertips.

2. Divide the meat evenly into 4 portions. Gently pat the meat into four 3-inch round patties. Don't make the patty so thick that it won't fit into your mouth when it's inside the bun. It's no fun to fight with your hamburger while trying to eat it.

3. Before you start to cook the hamburgers get all the condiments you want to serve out and ready. (Condiments are the mayonnaise, mustard, ketchup, etc.)

4. Put a large skillet on a stove burner and turn the heat to medium. After a minute, hold your hand, palm down, about 2 inches above the bottom of the skillet. If it feels good and warm the skillet is ready to use.

5. Put 1 tablespoon vegetable oil into the skillet and tilt and turn the skillet around so the oil coats the bottom.

6. Take a metal spatula, put a hamburger patty on it, and then slide the patty off the spatula into the skillet. Stand back while you do this so no oil spatters on you. Repeat until all 4 patties are in the skillet, with enough room around them so they aren't touching. Let them pan-fry for about 3 minutes, then turn them over with the metal spatula and let them cook another 2 minutes. They should be well browned on the outside and moist inside. Slide the skillet off the burner, and test the patties for doneness.

7. To test for doneness, cut a small slice into one of the hamburgers and pull gently apart with your knife so that you can see the color of the meat. If it is red-looking inside, the meat is rare. Some people like it that way, but if you find it too red, or even pink, for your taste and you want your hamburger well done, put it back in the pan and cook it another minute or two. When the hamburgers are done to your liking, place each one on a bun and let everyone add the condiments he or she likes.

MEATLOAF

SERVES 4

If you are making meatloaf for dinner, set the table and wash the greens for a salad (or prepare anything else you plan to have with the meatloaf) while it is baking. Then you will have everything ready so you can serve the meatloaf while it is hot and sit down and enjoy it. Remember that leftover meatloaf makes a wonderful sandwich the next day. It is just as delicious cold in a sandwich as it is hot on a plate.

1 POUND GROUND BEEF

1 EGG

1/3 CUP TOMATO KETCHUP

2 SLICES BREAD

1/4 CUP MILK

1 SMALL YELLOW ONION

1/2 TEASPOON SALT

1/4 TEASPOON PEPPER

EQUIPMENT LIST

LOAF PAN (8 1/2 BY 4 1/2 BY 2 1/2 INCHES, HOLDING 6 CUPS) OR ONE MEDIUM-SIZED BAKING DISH, HOLDING 6 CUPS

MIXING BOWL

SMALL BOWL

FORK

MEASURING CUP

PARING KNIFE OR 8-INCH SERRATED KNIFE

CUTTING BOARD

MEASURING SPOONS

KITCHEN TIMER

POT HOLDERS

THIN METAL SPATULA

4 SERVING PLATES

WHEN YOU USE THE OVEN

• Use soft, square potholders—the mitt-style potholder is not as protective. The mitts are usually too large and too stiff for children.

• When you open the oven door to check on something you are baking, don't pull the oven rack out, because this can cause the baking dish or pan to tilt forward and slide toward you.

• Don't leave the oven door open any longer than it takes you to comfortably check on the doneness of what you are baking. You don't need to be in a frantic rush when you open the oven, but remember that if you leave it open longer than you need to your oven will lose heat.

1. Turn the oven on to 350° F. You will need a loaf pan, or any medium-sized baking dish that will hold about 6 cups.

2. Put the ground beef into a mixing bowl and break it into pieces, handling it lightly. If you pack it down, press on it, and squeeze it firmly, it will be tough when it is baked. Handling it lightly and gently helps keep the meat moist and tender when it is baked.

3. Break the egg into a small bowl and stir it with a fork until it is all yellow and well mixed. Add 1/3 cup ketchup to the egg and stir to mix the two together. Pour the ketchup–egg mixture over the meat, but don't mix it in yet.

4. Tear the 2 slices of bread into bits about the size of a macaroni noodle, and put them in the bowl you used for the egg.

5. Sprinkle the 1/4 cup milk over the bread pieces, and then lightly toss them with your hands. Let the bread and milk sit a minute while you chop the onion.

6. First cut off the fuzzy little root end of the onion and then cut off the dry stem end. Peel off the papery outer skin, and then cut the onion in half from top to bottom. Put each half cut side down on a cutting board. Cut each half crosswise into 6 to 8 slices, then cut the slices across into 5 pieces. (You want to have little pieces of onion.) Add the chopped onion to the beef in the mixing bowl, but don't start mixing yet.

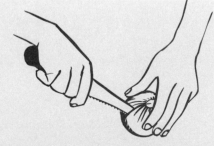

7. Now add to the meat the bread bits that have soaked up the milk, and sprinkle 1/2 teaspoon salt and 1/4 teaspoon pepper lightly over the beef and other ingredients.

8. Using your hands, gently mix all the ingredients together. This means lightly breaking up and mixing the beef, bread, ketchup and egg, onion, and salt and pepper together with your fingertips until you can see that everything is blended with everything else.

9. Gather up the beef mixture and put it into the loaf pan or baking dish. Pat it lightly so it is even on top. Put it in the oven and set the kitchen timer for 40 minutes.

10. Have your plates ready. When the timer bell rings, use pot holders to carefully remove the meatloaf from the oven and put it down on a heatproof surface. You can cut slices of meatloaf right out of the pan. Make them about 1 inch thick. Use a knife or a thin metal spatula to lift the slices out of the pan. Put the slices on the serving plates and eat while the meatloaf is still hot.

Chapter 4

RICE

1. HOW TO BOIL RICE AND HOW TO BAKE IT.
2. HOW TO MAKE A VEGETABLE STIR-FRY:

   PEELING GARLIC; CUTTING AND CHOPPING VEGETABLES

   ORGANIZING INGREDIENTS

   STIRRING AND TOSSING THE VEGETABLES AROUND IN THE SKILLET SO THEY COOK ON ALL SIDES.

Rice goes with just about everything—fish, chicken, pork, even beef. In this lesson you first learn two different methods of cooking rice and then you serve that rice with chopped vegetables cooked in a speedy way called "stir-frying." When you mix the stir-fried vegetables with the cooked rice, you will have a whole meal.

Rice is a kind of grass, like wheat or barley. It is usually grown in wet fields called paddies. You may have seen pictures of rice paddies, which look

like big green pools surrounded by raised grassy dikes. The water isn't very deep, so the farmers can wade in to harvest the crop.

The rice grains are the seeds of the plant. At harvest time, they are separated from their stalks. At the mill the rice kernels have their tough outer shell, or husk, rubbed off. Inside, there is a light brown layer around the kernel called bran. If this stays on, the rice is known as brown rice. If the bran is removed, you get white rice. Brown rice is good, but a little chewier than white rice, and it takes longer to cook.

The two kinds of white rice we see in markets are long-grain, which is dry and fluffy when cooked, and the short-grain type, which is moist and sticky when cooked. In this lesson you will use long-grain rice.

BOILED WHITE RICE

2 1/2 CUPS WATER

1 TEASPOON SALT

1 CUP LONG-GRAIN WHITE RICE

EQUIPMENT LIST

MEASURING CUP

**2- OR 3-QUART POT OR
SAUCEPAN WITH LID**

MEASURING SPOONS

LONG-HANDLED SPOON

KITCHEN TIMER

FORK

SLOTTED SPOON

POT HOLDERS

COLANDER OR STRAINER

SERVING BOWL

1. Pour the 2 1/2 cups water into a 2- or 3-quart pot or saucepan. Put the pot on the stove and turn the heat on to high. Add the 1 teaspoon salt.

2. Bring the water to a boil. ("Boil," you remember, means when lots of bubbles appear all over the top of the water.) Slowly pour the cup of rice into the boiling water. Stir with a long-handled spoon for just a second to get the rice separated and moving around. Turn the heat down to medium, but be sure the water continues to bubble. Set a timer for 15 minutes.

3. When the timer rings, you need to test the rice to see if it is done. Fish out a few grains of rice with a fork. Blow on them to cool them, then taste. If they are tender, the rice is done. If they still seem a little hard, boil another 2 or 3 minutes. Then turn off the heat.

4. If the pot feels too heavy to safely carry to the sink, remove the rice from the pot with a slotted spoon, holding each spoonful over the pan for a second to let any extra water drain off before you empty the rice into the serving bowl. If you can carry the pot, first put a colander or strainer in the sink. Use pot holders to carry the pot to the sink. Stand back a little and pour the water and rice into the colander so all the water drains away.

5. Either serve the rice at once or if you want to serve it a little later, dump out any water that's left in the pot, put the rice back into it, and cover with a lid so the rice stays hot until you are ready. It will keep warm for 10 to 15 minutes.

THE IMPORTANCE OF RICE

Rice is tiny but mighty. Every day, more people in this world eat rice than any other food. In fact, six out of ten people worldwide eat rice as the main part of every meal. It is so much a part of life in China that the Chinese greet each other by saying, "Have you eaten rice today?" This is a polite way of asking, "Are you well and happy?"

BAKED WHITE RICE

Sometimes it is easier to bake rice than to boil it. All you need to do is to put the rice, onion, and liquid into a casserole, then cover it and pop it into the oven, where it doesn't need any babysitting, and let it cook by itself for about 30 minutes. While it is quietly baking, you can set the table and make a salad.

EQUIPMENT LIST

PARING KNIFE OR 8-INCH SERRATED KNIFE

CUTTING BOARD

1 1/2-QUART (6 CUP) CASSEROLE (A ROUND, DEEP OVENPROOF DISH WITH TIGHT-FITTING LID)

MEDIUM-SIZED SAUCEPAN

MEASURING SPOONS

LONG-HANDLED SPOON

MEASURING CUP

POT HOLDERS

KITCHEN TIMER

1 SMALL (OR 1/2 MEDIUM-SIZED)* ONION

2 TABLESPOONS BUTTER

1 CUP LONG-GRAIN WHITE RICE

2 CUPS CHICKEN BROTH OR WATER

1/2 TEASPOON SALT

* See the box about using scraps on the opposite page.

1. See that the oven rack is at the middle level. Turn on the oven to 375° F.

2. Trim off the root end and peel away the outer papery skin of the onion and discard it. Chop the onion into small pieces.

3. Have a casserole ready that will hold 1 1/2 quarts and has a tight-fitting lid. Place a medium-sized saucepan on the stove, put in the 2 tablespoons butter, and turn the heat to medium. When the butter has melted, add the chopped onion. Stir it around with a long-handled spoon until the onion is a little soft, about 2 minutes. Add the 1 cup of rice to the saucepan. Keep stirring until all the grains of rice look shiny. Stir, cooking, for at least 1 minute. Pour the 2 cups chicken broth or water into the pot and add the 1/2 teaspoon salt. Stir again, and let the liquid start to boil.

4. As soon as bubbles appear, turn off the heat. Using pot holders, carefully pour the rice and liquid from the saucepan into the casserole. Put the lid on the casserole and, using pot holders, carefully place the casserole in the oven on the middle rack. Set a timer for 30 minutes.

5. After 30 minutes, carefully take the casserole out of the oven, using pot holders. Remove the lid, standing back a little, away from the steam. All the liquid should be absorbed by the rice. Take out a spoonful of rice, blow on it to cool it a little, and taste for doneness. If it is a little hard when you chew it, put the lid back on and bake the rice for 5 to 10 more minutes. If you aren't serving the rice right away, keep the lid on after you take the casserole out of the oven.

SAVING SCRAPS

When you are using only half an onion, wrap the other half tightly in plastic wrap and store in the refrigerator. Do the same with any part of a vegetable you're not using right away. There will always be a use for them.

VEGETABLE STIR-FRY WITH RICE

SERVES 3 TO 4

1 CARROT

1 ZUCCHINI

1 GREEN BELL PEPPER

1 SCALLION (GREEN ONION)

1 LARGE CLOVE GARLIC

4 TABLESPOONS OLIVE OIL

1 TABLESPOON SOY SAUCE

3 CUPS BOILED OR BAKED WHITE RICE

   (PAGES 30, 32)*

SALT

*If the boiled or baked white rice is cold or barely warm, put it in a casserole with a lid. Turn the oven on to 350°. Put the casserole in the oven before you start peeling the vegetables for the stir-fry. It will take you about 20 minutes to make the stir-fry, which should be just enough time to get the rice hot.

1. Cut off both ends of the carrot, then peel it with a vegetable peeler. Slice the carrot into rounds about as thick as a nickel. Rinse the zucchini, then cut off both ends of the zucchini, then slice it into rounds the same thickness as the carrot.

2. Rinse the bell pepper, then cut it in half lengthwise and cut off and throw away the stem. Scrape out the seeds and cut off the white ribs. Cut the pepper into thin strips. Then bunch the strips together and cut into small pieces. Put them in a small bowl.

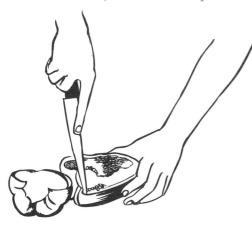

3. Cut off the little roots at the white end of the scallion, and cut off all but 1 inch of the green tops. Then slice the white and pale-green part thinly. Put the pieces in the bowl with the pepper.

4. Put the clove of garlic on the cutting surface. Hold a small skillet firmly by its handle and give the garlic clove a whack with the flat bottom of the skillet so that it is smashed a little, but not totally demolished. This loosens the peel so that it almost falls off. Remove and discard the peel and chop the garlic clove into tiny pieces. Add the garlic to the bowl with the bell pepper and scallion.

5. Put a medium-sized skillet on the stove and turn the heat to medium. Have a large serving bowl nearby. When the skillet is hot, it is ready to use. To test, put your hand, palm side down, about 2 inches above the skillet. If it feels hot, the skillet is ready. Pour in 2 tablespoons olive oil. Stand back and add the carrots. If they sizzle or pop, turn the heat down. Stir the carrots with a long-handled spoon for about 2 minutes, holding the handle of the skillet in your other hand to keep the skillet from moving.

6. Pour the remaining 2 tablespoons olive oil into the skillet. Add the zucchini and stir for a few seconds. Toss in the chopped pepper, scallion, and garlic. Cook, stirring, for another minute. Turn off the heat.

7. Using pot holders, hold the skillet handle with both hands and pour all the vegetables from the skillet into the serving bowl. Use your spoon to scrape the skillet clean. Sprinkle the 1 tablespoon soy sauce over the vegetables. Toss with the spoon. Add 3 cups warm boiled or baked rice and stir again to mix the rice with the vegetables. Taste and add a little salt if the dish needs it. Stir again and then serve right away.

Chapter 5

EGGS

1. HOW TO CRACK AN EGG.
2. HOW TO FRY EGGS "SUNNY SIDE UP" AND "OVER EASY" (TURNING THEM).
3. HOW TO FRY AN EGG OVER A PIECE OF TOAST WITH A HOLE CUT OUT OF THE MIDDLE.
4. HOW TO SCRAMBLE EGGS GENTLY.
5. HOW TO MAKE AND FILL AN OMELET.
6. HOW TO FRY BACON.
7. HOW TO GRATE CHEESE.

An egg is a marvel inside a perfect oval shell. It has the strength and power to lift and lighten cakes, pop popovers, thicken sauces, and hold cookies and custards together. Eggs by themselves make delicious lunch or supper dishes.

Eggs are tricky until you discover some of their secrets. For example, if a bit of eggshell falls into the bowl when you are cracking an egg, use an-

other piece of shell to fish it out. The two pieces of shell will stick together like magnets.

Eggs perform best when they are treated gently. Don't fry, scramble, poach, bake, or even boil eggs over high heat. High heat turns an egg white tough and rubbery, and the yolk becomes unpleasant to taste. Eggs also don't like to be forgotten. When frying, scrambling, or poaching eggs, stand right by them. Watch and time them so they don't overcook. It is important to work quickly and keep your eye on your eggs!

Eggs are strong, but they are delicate, too. When you crack open an egg, sometimes a sharp piece of shell pricks the yellow yolk and punctures it like a balloon. Then the yolk goes flat and the yellow part runs into the white. If you are making scrambled eggs or an omelet, it won't matter, because you'll be stirring the yolk and white together anyway. But if you're going to fry an egg, you want the yolk to be separate from the white, so you have to be careful cracking the egg open.

FRIED EGG

1 EGG

2 TEASPOONS BUTTER

SALT AND PEPPER

EQUIPMENT LIST

SMALL BOWL

SMALL SKILLET

METAL SPATULA

PLATE

1. The way to crack open an eggshell is to give the fat middle part of the egg a light rap against the rim of a bowl to crack the shell. (Don't whack it too hard against the bowl or you will break the yolk of the egg and it will run into the white.)

Then, holding the egg with both hands over the bowl, use your thumbs to gently pull the crack apart. (Don't stick your thumb too far into the crack or, again, you'll puncture the yolk.) Make the crack wide enough so the shell opens up and the white and yolk slip easily out of the eggshell and fall into the bowl. Again, be gentle as you let the egg fall and don't hold it too high above the bowl or the yolk will break.

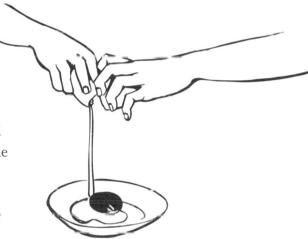

MEASURING A SKILLET

The way to tell the size of a skillet called for in a recipe is to measure with a ruler across the top of the skillet at the widest part. That is the pan's diameter and it defines the size. A small skillet is about 5 to 6 inches in diameter, a medium skillet 7 to 9 inches, and a large skillet 10 to 12 inches.

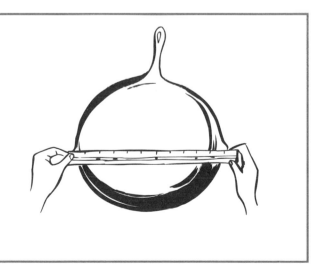

2. Set a small skillet on the stove burner. Turn the heat on medium-low and put the 2 teaspoons butter in the skillet. Don't walk away. As soon as the butter has melted, tilt and tip the skillet a little—up, down, and around, so the butter covers the bottom of the skillet.

3. Set the skillet back on the burner and slide the egg gently from the bowl into the skillet. Lightly salt and pepper the egg.

4. As soon as the white part of the egg turns from shiny and clear to firm and white, the egg is done "sunny side up." "Sunny side up" means it is fried only on one side. Many people like their eggs fried this way because the eggs are more tender and delicate than those fried on both sides.

5. When you fry eggs on both sides they are called eggs "over easy." If you want your egg over easy, slide a metal spatula under the egg, wiggling it a little as you slide. Then lift the spatula and gently turn it over so that the cooked side of the egg is up (facing you). Let it fry only a few seconds more.

6. Whether you have fried it "sunny side up" or "over easy," when the egg is done lift it out with the spatula and slide it onto a plate. Eat it while it is hot.

KNOTHOLE EGG

SERVES 1

1 SLICE BREAD

1 EGG

1 TABLESPOON BUTTER

SALT AND PEPPER

EQUIPMENT LIST

TOASTER

2-INCH ROUND COOKIE CUTTER
    OR A SMALL GLASS

SMALL BOWL

SMALL SKILLET WITH COVER

SPOON

METAL SPATULA

PLATE

1. Toast the bread lightly in a toaster. Using a 2-inch round cookie cutter or a small glass, cut a hole out of the center of the slice of toast. Discard the little round piece of bread—or eat it up.

2. Hold the egg over a small bowl and give the fat middle part of the eggshell a light tap on the edge of the bowl. You should have made a crack in the middle of the shell. Hold the egg over the bowl with both hands (not too high up) and use your thumbs to pull the crack apart wide enough to let the whole egg slip into the bowl.

3. Put a small skillet on the stove. Turn the heat to medium-low. Add the tablespoon of butter. When it melts, lift the skillet a little and tilt it all around so the butter coats the bottom. Put the toast in the skillet. Now pour the egg from the bowl into the hole in the bread so the yolk falls into the hole. The white will run over the bread, which is what it is meant to do. (Have a spoon nearby, so if the yolk misses the hole you can gently shove it in with the spoon.)

4. Turn the heat as low as possible. Sprinkle the egg with salt and pepper. Cover the skillet and cook for about 1 1/2 minutes. Then take off the cover, turn the toast and egg over with a metal spatula, and cook the other side for just a few seconds more, uncovered. Slide the spatula under the bread-and-egg and carefully lift it out of the skillet, put it on a plate, and eat it while it is hot.

SCRAMBLED EGGS

SERVES 1

Scrambled eggs are made by mixing eggs together in a bowl with a little water (water is much better than milk), then pouring them into a skillet, and continuing to stir them as they cook. Very soon you will see the eggs forming into soft, creamy lumps. Some people like their scrambled eggs creamy and moist, and some like them firmer. It is easy to cook them either way as long as you stay right by the stove and watch carefully so that when they are done to your liking you can remove them from the heat quickly.

2 EGGS

2 TABLESPOONS WATER

SALT AND PEPPER

2 TEASPOONS BUTTER

EQUIPMENT LIST

SMALL BOWL

MEASURING SPOONS

FORK OR WHISK

MEDIUM SKILLET

PLATE

1. Crack the 2 eggs into a small bowl. Add the 2 tablespoons water. Hold the bowl firmly with one hand while you beat the eggs and water together with a fork or a whisk until

the white and yolk are mixed together and the mixture is all yellow. Lightly sprinkle the eggs with salt and pepper and beat again.

2. Put a medium skillet on a stove burner. Turn the heat on to medium-low. Add the 2 teaspoons butter to the skillet, and when they're melted, lift the skillet a little off the burner and tilt and turn it all around so the butter covers the bottom.

3. Pour the egg mixture into the skillet. Holding the skillet handle with one hand the whole time, gently and slowly stir the eggs with a fork, being sure to scrape the bottom of the skillet with the flat part of the fork as you stir. As parts of the eggs get firm, push them to the sides of the skillet and let the parts that are still liquid run over the bottom of the skillet. Keep stirring until the eggs are cooked the way you want them. Don't leave even for a second; the cooking goes very fast. Scoop the eggs onto a plate and enjoy eating them while they're hot.

GRATING CHEESE

To grate cheese, put a piece of waxed paper about the size of a sheet of paper towel (or notebook paper) on the counter. Stand a grater in the center

of the paper and start rubbing a big piece of firm cheese against the sharp holes. If you have a grater with several different sized holes, use the larger

holes. You'll find it easier. (Big chunks of cheese are easier to grate than small chunks.) Have a measuring cup nearby so you can see if you have grated about the right amount. Measure when you think you have enough: Pick up the waxed paper and pour the cheese into the measuring cup. If you need a little more, continue grating some over the waxed paper; if you have too much store it in a small jar in the refrigerator to use some other time.

Building a strawberry shortcake

Saucing and tossing the pasta

BACON CHEESE OMELET

SERVES 1

Omelets are made with eggs that are stirred together, poured into a skillet, and cooked quickly to make a soft, yellow blanket that is wrapped around a tasty filling. Omelets are similar to scrambled eggs, but scrambled eggs are stirred as they cook to form creamy little lumps, and omelets aren't stirred, so they remain smooth and flat—thus easier to fold around a filling. Omelets are a blessing to cooks who want to fix a fast, simple lunch or supper and have very little food on hand. A few eggs and some cheese or other flavorful tidbits, such as cooked ham, can quickly solve the problem.

ABOUT 1/4 CUP GRATED CHEDDAR CHEESE

  (SEE BOX)

2 STRIPS BACON

2 EGGS

2 TABLESPOONS WATER

SALT AND PEPPER

EQUIPMENT LIST

WAXED PAPER

CHEESE GRATER

MEASURING CUPS

8- OR 9-INCH SKILLET

FORK

PARING KNIFE OR 8-INCH
  SERRATED KNIFE

2 SMALL BOWLS

MEASURING SPOONS

SMALL METAL SPATULA

PLATE

1. Have the 1/4 cup cheese grated and ready to use by the stove.

2. Put the 2 bacon strips side by side in an 8- or 9-inch skillet. Turn the heat on to medium-high. Have a fork ready to use when it's time to turn the bacon over. Bacon sometimes sizzles and pops a little, so don't stand too close to the stove. As the bacon fries, it tends to curl a little. Flatten the bacon by pressing it down with the back of the fork. When the bacon loses its raw look and becomes slightly golden, turn each strip over, and again press the bacon flat with the fork. Let the bacon cook until it has lost its soft, floppy texture, and is firmer and browned. Have a paper towel on a surface nearby, so you can take out the strips of bacon and put them on the paper towel to soak up the fat. Turn the heat off, and slide the skillet off the burner so it cools down a bit. Pat the bacon with the paper towel to remove excess fat. Cut the bacon into small pieces and put the pieces into a small bowl. Dump the grated cheese into the bowl with the bacon.

3. Pour the bacon fat from the skillet into a small bowl. Measure 1 tablespoon of the fat from the bowl and put it back into the skillet, discarding the rest of the fat.

4. Crack the eggs into a small mixing bowl. Add the 2 tablespoons water to the eggs and stir briskly with a fork until the whites and yolks are blended and the mixture is all yellow. Season lightly with salt and pepper, then set the eggs near the stove. Have the bowl of chopped bacon and grated cheese near the stove too, so they are ready when you need to add them to the eggs, and have the plate that you will serve your omelet on nearby. You must work quickly when you cook eggs, because it doesn't take long to cook them.

5. Put the skillet back on the stove, and turn the heat to medium. Lift the skillet a little and tilt and turn it so the bacon fat coats the bottom.

6. Hold your hand, palm down, about 2 inches above the skillet. When it feels warm, slide the eggs into the skillet. Give the skillet a shake to level the eggs. In less than a minute you will see

the edges lose their liquid shine and become set. Holding the skillet handle with one hand, use a fork with the other to pull the edges toward the center of the pan in 3 or 4 places; this lets the runny center of the omelet flow out to the edge of the skillet, where the heat will set it. Keep pulling the edges toward the center in several places, tilting the pan to let the egg run out to finish cooking. The whole procedure should not take more than a minute or two. When most of the egg is firm, sprinkle the bacon bits and grated cheese over half the omelet (the half farthest from the skillet handle). Hold the handle with one hand and with a spatula in the other hand gently lift the unfilled half of the omelet and fold it over the filled part. Slide the finished omelet onto a plate and eat it while it is hot.

AVOCADO AND SOUR CREAM OMELET

SERVES 1

Sara Connett has been one of my students for almost two years, and this is her favorite omelet. I promised her I would put it in this book so you could make it too.

EQUIPMENT LIST

PARING KNIFE OR 8-INCH
    SERRATED KNIFE

CUTTING BOARD

2 SMALL BOWLS

MEASURING SPOONS

SPOON

FORK

8- OR 9-INCH SKILLET

METAL SPATULA

PLATE

1 AVOCADO

2 TABLESPOONS SOUR CREAM

2 EGGS

2 TABLESPOONS WATER

SALT AND PEPPER

1 TABLESPOON BUTTER

1. Cut the avocado in half lengthwise. Gently twist each half until they come apart. You are going to use only half the avocado, so wrap the half with the pit tightly in plastic wrap and refrigerate for future use. Peel the other half and cut into 8 slices. Cut the slices into small pieces.

2. Put the chopped avocado in a small bowl and add the 2 tablespoons sour cream. Stir the mixture gently with a spoon. Put the bowl next to the stove so the filling will be handy when you're ready to put it into the omelet.

3. Break the 2 eggs into another small bowl, add 2 tablespoons water, and stir briskly with a fork to mix together yolk and white; season lightly with salt and pepper. Put an 8- or 9-inch skillet on the stove over medium heat and add the 1 tablespoon butter. As it melts, lift the skillet a little and tilt and turn it so the butter coats the bottom.

4. When the butter foams a little, slide the eggs into the skillet. Give the skillet a shake to level the eggs. After a few seconds, when the edges of the egg have started to set, hold the skillet firmly and with the other hand use a fork to pull the edges of the egg mixture toward the center and allow the runny, uncooked egg to spread out to the edge of the skillet. Keep pulling the edges toward the center of the skillet. After a minute or so, when most of the egg is firm, spread the avocado and sour cream over half the omelet, fold the un-filled half over the filled part with a spatula, and slide the omelet onto a serving plate.

Chapter 6

PANCAKES and POPOVERS

WHAT YOU LEARN MAKING

PANCAKES and POPOVERS

1. HOW TO MIX A BATTER.

2. HOW TO TEST THE HEAT OF YOUR SKILLET.

3. HOW TO COOK PANCAKES ON TOP OF THE STOVE (AND OBSERVING THE RISING POWER OF BAKING POWDER).

4. HOW TO GREASE BAKING CUPS.

5. HOW TO CHECK POPOVERS FOR DONENESS (AND OBSERVING THE RISING POWER OF EGGS).

6. HOW TO LET STEAM ESCAPE FROM THE POPOVERS.

7. HOW TO UNMOLD THE POPOVERS.

Pancakes and popovers make everyone happy. Even crabby people smile when you put pancakes or popovers on their plate. They make me happy too, and I'm not sure why. Sunday morning breakfast is when pancakes appear, but popovers can pop up any old time—for breakfast, lunch, dinner, or eleven o'clock in the morning. And, as a treat, if you have been out-of-sorts all day, fix some pancakes for supper and just see how cheerful you begin to feel. If you follow the recipes carefully you will never have to say, "Pardon my pancakes" or "Pardon my popovers" to anyone.

How to Measure Ingredients

Measuring accurately is very important in cooking, especially in baking. Too much flour or too much milk can ruin a cake. For all of these baking recipes to turn out well, the ingredients must be measured in *level* spoonfuls and cupfuls.

To use measuring spoons, select the size measuring spoon that your recipe calls for, scoop it into a dry ingredient, such as baking powder or sugar or salt, and then lift a generous amount out of the container. The spoon will be holding more than you need, so with the back of a knife or your finger scrape off whatever excess is mounded over the top to make a smooth, level surface.

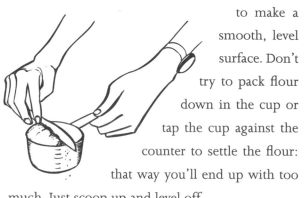

A warning: Don't get mixed up between tablespoons and teaspoons. To remember that a tablespoon is the bigger size, just think that a table is bigger than a cup of tea.

To measure cupfuls of dry ingredients such as flour or sugar, use one of the metal or plastic measuring cups that come in a set of four sizes: 1 cup, 1/2 cup, 1/3 cup, and 1/4 cup. Selecting the size called for in the recipe, dip the cup into the flour or sugar and scoop up a generous amount, so that you'll have a little hill above the rim of the cup. Then with the back of a knife scrape off the excess to make a smooth, level surface. Don't try to pack flour down in the cup or tap the cup against the counter to settle the flour: that way you'll end up with too much. Just scoop up and level off.

To measure cupfuls of wet ingredients such as milk or water, use a clear glass measuring cup with a pouring spout. Pour in whatever amount of liquid is called for, let's say 1/2 cup, then place the measuring cup on a flat surface and stoop down so the cup is at eye level. When you're looking straight at the side of the glass, you can check and see that your liquid comes exactly to the 1/2 cup mark printed on the measuring cup. If it doesn't, pour off a little of the liquid or add more as needed.

Glass measuring cups come in different sizes—from 1 cup up to 8 cups.

PANCAKES

MAKES ABOUT SIXTEEN 3-INCH PANCAKES

1/2 STICK (4 TABLESPOONS) BUTTER

1 CUP MILK

2 EGGS

1 1/4 CUPS FLOUR

1 TABLESPOON SUGAR

2 TEASPOONS BAKING POWDER

1/2 TEASPOON SALT

2 TABLESPOONS VEGETABLE OIL

TO GO WITH THE PANCAKES:

BUTTER AT ROOM TEMPERATURE

MAPLE SYRUP

EQUIPMENT LIST

MEASURING CUPS

SMALL SAUCEPAN

MIXING BOWL

MEASURING SPOONS

FORK

LARGE SPOON

LARGE-SIZED SKILLET

METAL SPATULA

1. If your butter is very cold, cut it into 4 or 5 pieces so it will melt more quickly in the milk. Put the butter and 1 cup milk into a small saucepan and set the saucepan on a stove burner. Turn the heat on to medium. It will only take a minute or two for the milk to get hot enough to melt the butter, so stay by the stove, watch, and stir the milk mixture often. When the milk is hot and the butter is melted, take the saucepan off the burner and let the mixture cool a little.

2. Crack the 2 eggs into a mixing bowl. Beat the eggs together with a fork until the yolks and whites are blended and the eggs become all yellow. Before you add the milk and butter to the eggs, be sure the mixture has cooled. Test it by poking your finger quickly in and out of the saucepan to check. If the mixture is barely warm, add it to the eggs. If it is still hot, let it cool a little longer and then add it to the eggs. Stir the eggs and milk mixture together.

3. Put the 1 1/4 cups flour, 1 tablespoon sugar, 2 teaspoons baking powder, and 1/2 teaspoon salt into a mixing bowl. Stir the flour mixture with a fork, going round and round in the bowl so everything gets mixed together nicely.

4. Add the flour mixture (the dry ingredients) to the egg mixture (the wet ingredients). Stir everything together with a large spoon. The minute you see that the batter (this uncooked mixture) looks moist with lots of lumps, kind of like soupy cottage cheese, stop stirring! If you stir too much, the pancakes will be tough.

5. Spread 1 teaspoon of the vegetable oil all over the bottom of a large skillet, using your fingers or a piece of paper towel. Put the skillet on a burner and turn the heat to medium-high. In a few seconds, sprinkle a few drops of water on the bottom of the skillet, and if they dance, pop, and sputter, the skillet is hot. The first pancake you make is a test pancake to get the feel of how hot the skillet is, and how long it will take to cook the pancake on both sides. Drop one large spoonful of batter into the skillet.

As the pancake cooks, watch for tiny bubbles forming on the top and sides. When you see the bubbles all over the top side, this usually means the pancake is ready to turn over. Slide a metal spatula under the pancake and gently turn it over. It should look golden on top. If it looks very brown, turn the heat down a little. Let it cook a few more seconds, then slide the metal spatula again under the pancake, and lift the edge up so you can look and see if the bottom is golden. If it is, remove the pancake from the skillet onto a plate and cut into the middle. If it isn't runny it is done.

6. Now you are ready to get serious about making your pancakes. Have everything ready to go— butter, syrup, plates, knives, forks, napkins— so you can make 3 or 4 pancakes at one time, which is a good serving for each person. Make the pancakes just as you did with the test pancake, this time dropping 3 or 4 large spoonfuls (one at a time) of the batter around the pan, not touching. As you remove the pancakes from the skillet, serve them immediately and finally serve yourself. Then you can make more pancakes for those with hearty appetites. Or your friends can take a turn at being a cook and try their hand at making pancakes.

BAKING POWDER:
THE BIGGEST LITTLE THING IN BAKING

Baking powder used to be called "The Biggest Little Thing in Baking" because it takes so little to do so much. Two teaspoons of baking powder can make pancakes light. Two teaspoons can lift biscuits high and can make a cake big and airy.

When baking powder is mixed into a liquid or a moist dough, tiny air bubbles start to form, just like the fizz in soda pop. Those bubbles expand when they're hot, which is why a cake rises in the oven. And when the cake firms up, the bubbles are trapped inside, keeping the cake light. Baking powder performs the same amazing trick in pancakes, biscuits, shortcake, cookies, and certain kinds of breads.

Sometimes you see baking powder described as a "leaven" or "leavener" in cookbooks, which simply means "to raise or make light."

WHY DO PANCAKES AND POPOVERS RISE?

Pancakes puff up gently when they are cooked in the skillet, and popovers rise when they're baked in the oven, changing miraculously from wet white batter to big golden balloons.

The magic of what you see happening is really a simple scientific principle at work. When certain ingredients are combined and then heated they create bubbles that lift the batters and make them light and airy. Baking powder and moisture make bubbles when they meet in the pancake batter, and egg power alone pushes the popovers higher and higher as they bake in a hot oven. In case you wonder what makes the bubbles stay in the pancakes and popovers, it is heat—the heat in the skillet and the heat from the oven.

POPOVERS

MAKES 6 POPOVERS

Don't use muffin tins to bake popovers. Use individual Pyrex cups or popover pans, if you have them (see picture below), because the secret to making high and mighty popovers is to bake them in containers that are separate, so that the oven heat completely surrounds each individual popover container.

BUTTER TO GREASE THE POPOVER CONTAINERS

3 LARGE EGGS

1 CUP MILK

1 CUP FLOUR

1/2 TEASPOON SALT

TO GO WITH THE POPOVERS:

> **BUTTER AT ROOM TEMPERATURE**
>
> **STRAWBERRY OR OTHER JAM**

EQUIPMENT LIST

POPOVER CONTAINERS (INDIVIDUAL 3/4-CUP PYREX CUPS OR SPECIAL POPOVER PANS—SEE ILLUSTRATION)

MIXING BOWL

WHISK

MEASURING CUPS

MEASURING SPOONS

4-CUP MEASURING CUP OR PITCHER

BAKING SHEET

KITCHEN TIMER

POT HOLDERS

PARING KNIFE OR 8-INCH SERRATED KNIFE

1. Turn the oven on to 400° F. Make sure the rack is in the middle of the oven. Grease the insides of 6 popover containers with a little piece of butter, using your fingers or a piece of paper towel.

2. Crack 3 eggs into a mixing bowl. Beat the eggs briskly with a whisk, just until the yolks and whites become all yellow. (Beating is more vigorous than stirring and you do it very fast.)

3. Add the 1 cup milk and stir until the eggs and milk are mixed together.

4. Add the 1 cup flour and 1/2 teaspoon salt to the egg mixture in the bowl and beat the batter with the whisk until it is smooth and the lumps have disappeared.

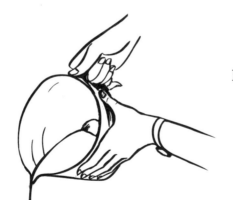

5. Pour the popover batter into a 4-cup measuring cup or pitcher, so it's easy for you to pour the batter into the popover containers.

6. Fill each popover container about half full of batter.

7. If you are using individual Pyrex cups, place them 2 inches apart on a baking sheet and put the baking sheet into the center of the oven. Or put the popover pans in the oven.

8. Set the kitchen timer for 25 minutes. When the timer bell goes off, start checking the popovers. Popovers baked in Pyrex cups usually take about 25 to 35 minutes. They should stand tall and be puffed up, looking like giant golden balloons. When they are nice and brown on top, they are done.

9. When the popovers are done, remove them from the oven with pot holders. Quickly pierce each popover in 3 or 4 places around the top and sides with the pointed tip of a paring knife. The holes let the steam escape, which helps prevent the popovers from falling, or flattening out. (By doing this trick of piercing the popovers quickly, you can reheat them, if you don't eat them all up at once, and they will again puff up a little.) Remove the popovers from their pan or cups. If they don't come out easily, run a knife around the sides of each popover. Eat them hot with butter and strawberry jam.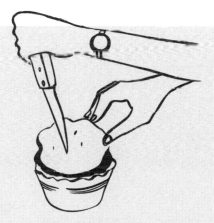

Chapter 7

BAKING POWDER BISCUITS

BISCUITS and SHORTCAKE

1. HOW TO MIX SHORTENING AND FLOUR TOGETHER WITH YOUR FINGERS.
2. HOW TO KNEAD AND CUT OUT BISCUIT DOUGH.
3. HOW TO BAKE BISCUITS AND SHORTCAKE AND TEST FOR DONENESS.
4. HOW TO PREPARE STRAWBERRIES.
5. HOW TO WHIP CREAM.
6. HOW TO SPLIT SHORTCAKES, FILL THEM, AND TOP THEM.

Here is a "two for the price of one" lesson. First you will learn how to make baking powder biscuits—those light, golden biscuits served warm with honey and butter that everyone loves but few people make at home these days. You'll notice how they will disappear faster than you can say, "Pass the

biscuits, please." Then, by changing the biscuit recipe a little, you'll learn how to make a very good dessert: strawberry shortcake.

This lesson helps you understand oven baking. Sometimes ovens are a little hotter or colder than they're supposed to be, so your biscuits might bake a little faster or slower than the recipe says they should. That's why it is so important to check your biscuits when baking—they may be done sooner than you think. Practice makes perfect. If you make them several times in the weeks after you first tackle this lesson, you will get better each time. It is as though your hands memorize the recipe.

BAKING POWDER BISCUITS

MAKES ABOUT SIXTEEN 2-INCH BISCUITS

When you learn to mix flour and shortening together with your fingers, you will get to know how dough should feel. You will use the same technique to make a good pie crust (see pages 140–42) and many other baked things.

EQUIPMENT LIST

- 8- OR 9-INCH SQUARE BAKING PAN
- MEASURING CUPS
- LARGE MIXING BOWL
- MEASURING SPOONS
- FORK
- SPOON
- ROLLING PIN
- 2-INCH ROUND COOKIE CUTTER, A SMALL GLASS, OR A KNIFE
- KITCHEN TIMER
- POT HOLDERS
- METAL SPATULA

1/3 CUP VEGETABLE SHORTENING, PLUS A LITTLE MORE FOR GREASING THE PAN (SEE STEP 3 FOR MEASURING IT)

2 CUPS ALL-PURPOSE FLOUR (SEE PAGE 56 FOR MEASURING), PLUS MORE FOR DUSTING YOUR HANDS, THE BOARD, AND THE ROLLING PIN

1 TABLESPOON BAKING POWDER (SEE PAGE 56 FOR MEASURING)

1 TEASPOON SALT

1 CUP MILK

TO GO WITH THE BISCUITS:

BUTTER

HONEY OR JAM

1. Turn the oven on to 450° F. Make sure the rack is in the center of the oven. With your fingers scoop up a little vegetable shortening and smear it all around the bottom and sides of an 8- or 9-inch square baking pan. It will leave a thin layer of grease that will prevent the dough from sticking to the pan when baking.

2. Put the 2 cups flour in a large mixing bowl. Add the 1 tablespoon baking powder and the 1 teaspoon salt. Use a fork to stir the ingredients around 5 or 6 times so they will be well mixed.

3. With a spoon, scoop up shortening and press it into a 1/3 cup measuring cup, pack-ing it down firmly and leveling it off. (Don't worry about being precise; a little more or less doesn't matter in this case.) Use your fingers to scrape the shortening from the cup and dump it into the bowl with the flour.

4. Flour your hands, then turn the shortening around in the flour to make it less sticky. Break the shortening into 4 or 5 small pieces and coat the pieces with the flour in the bowl.

5. With your fingers, lightly rub the shortening and flour together for about a minute to make little lumps. This is how you do it: Plunge your fingers into the bowl and take up a small amount of flour and shortening, rubbing the mixture between your thumbs and fingers and letting the flour and shortening, now lumped together, fall back into the bowl. Repeat, lifting the loose flour up to the top with your hands and rubbing shortening into it to make more little lumps. Work lightly with your fingertips—no need to squeeze the dough. When most of the flour and shortening is combined and in little lumps, you have mixed enough.

6. Add the 1 cup milk to the flour and shortening mixture. Stir the dough with a fork. (A dough is any mixture of flour, liquid, and other ingredients that is stiff enough to shape with your hands.) It will be sticky, but don't worry—you'll be able to work with the dough. Being moist and therefore sticky is what makes these biscuits rise high and taste tender.

SHORTENING

"Shortening" is the word cooks use for the fat they bake with. Not only is "vegetable shortening" a shortening, but also butter, margarine, and vegetable oils; all of them have the same effect in baking. Dough made with flour mixed with shortening turns golden and tender when it bakes. When you use shortening to grease a pan, it makes the surface slippery so that what you bake won't stick to the pan.

7. Sprinkle 2 tablespoons flour on a large board or counter top. Spread the flour in a circle.

8. Flour your hands again, then scoop the dough out of the bowl and onto the floured surface. Knead the dough about 10 times to make it a little easier to handle and roll out. Here's how to knead: Press down on the dough with the palms of your hands, pushing it away from you. Fold the dough back toward yourself, then give it a quarter-turn. Keep pushing, folding, and turning the dough 10 times.

9. Pat the dough into a circle, or roll it out with a rolling pin into a circle, about 8 inches across and 1/2 inch thick—about as thick as a thick slice of bread. Now you can cut your biscuits any size you like. I use a 2-inch round cookie cutter. Press it onto the dough firmly at the edge of the circle, and then lift it off—you'll have a perfectly cut circle of dough. Repeat, cutting the next circle close to the first so that you won't have too much leftover dough. If you don't have a cookie cutter, you can use the rim of a small drinking glass to cut out your biscuits. You could also pat the dough into a square and use a knife to cut square biscuits. If you are making round biscuits, you will have some dough left after you have cut out the first biscuits. Pat the leftover dough into an-other circle the same thickness as before and cut out as many biscuits as you can.

10. Place the biscuits, touching one another, in the baking pan. Put the biscuit pan in the center of the oven. These biscuits almost always take 15 to 18 minutes to bake, but set the timer for 12 minutes and when it goes off check the biscuits. If they have already turned golden brown on top, they are done. If not, let them bake a few minutes more.

11. Using pot holders, remove the baking pan from the oven. Put the pan down on a heatproof surface and wait 3 minutes for the biscuits to cool a little. Then they should be cool enough to lift right off. If you want to take them out of the pan when they're fresh out of the oven, slide a spatula under each one and place it on a plate. Eat the biscuits while they are warm, with butter and honey.

SHORTCAKE

MAKES 4 SHORTCAKES

This dough is almost exactly the same as baking powder biscuit dough, except that it has a little sugar added to it. Instead of making round biscuits, this time you cut the dough into squares. Also, by not letting the cut pieces of dough touch one another when you put them on the baking sheet, the biscuits will be brown and crispy on all sides when baked. This recipe makes half the dough used for the biscuits, but it is enough for 4 good-sized shortcakes.

EQUIPMENT LIST

BAKING SHEET

MEASURING CUPS

MEASURING SPOONS

LARGE MIXING BOWL

FORK

PARING KNIFE OR 8-INCH
   SERRATED KNIFE

KITCHEN TIMER

POT HOLDERS

3 TABLESPOONS VEGETABLE SHORTENING, PLUS A

   LITTLE MORE FOR GREASING THE PAN

1 CUP ALL-PURPOSE FLOUR, PLUS MORE FOR

   DUSTING YOUR HANDS AND THE BOARD

2 TEASPOONS BAKING POWDER

1/4 TEASPOON SALT

2 TABLESPOONS SUGAR

1/2 CUP MILK

1. Turn the oven on to 450° F. Make sure the rack is in the center of the oven. With your fingers or a paper towel scoop up a little vegetable shortening and grease a baking sheet.

2. Put the 1 cup flour in a large mixing bowl. Add 2 teaspoons baking powder, 1/4 teaspoon salt, and 2 tablespoons sugar. Use a fork to stir the ingredients around 5 or 6 times so they're well mixed.

3. Measure out 3 tablespoons of shortening and add to the bowl with the flour.

4. Flour your hands, then turn the shortening around in the flour to make it less sticky. Break the shortening into 4 or 5 small pieces and roll them around in the flour mixture to coat them so they are easy to handle.

5. With your fingers, lightly rub the shortening and flour together for about a minute to make little lumps: Plunge your fingers into the bowl and take up a small amount of flour and shortening, rubbing the mixture between your thumbs and fingers and letting the flour and shortening, now lumped together, fall back into the bowl. Repeat, lifting the loose flour up to the top with your hands and rubbing shortening into it to make more lumps. Work lightly. When most of the flour and shortening is combined in little lumps, you have mixed enough.

6. Add the 1/2 cup milk to the flour and shortening mixture. Stir the dough with a fork. It will be sticky.

7. Sprinkle 2 tablespoons flour on a large board or countertop. Spread the flour in a circle.

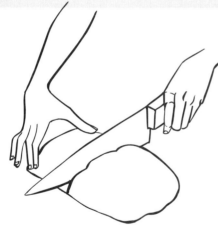

8. Flour your hands again, then scoop the dough out of the bowl and put it onto the floured board. Knead the dough about 10 times: Press down on the dough with the palms of your hands, pushing it away from you. Fold the dough back toward yourself, then give it a quarter-turn. Sprinkle a little more flour over the dough if it gets too sticky to handle easily. Keep pushing, folding, and turning the dough 10 times.

9. Pat the dough into a square about 5 inches on each side. Keep the edges as thick as the middle so the shortcakes will bake evenly. Cut the square into 4 equal square biscuits. Place the shortcakes on the baking sheet about an inch apart.

10. Put the baking sheet in the middle of the oven. The shortcakes almost always take 15 to 18 minutes to bake, but set the timer for 12 minutes, and when it goes off, start checking them. If they have already turned golden brown on top, they are done. If not, let them bake a few more minutes.

11. Use pot holders to remove the baking sheet from the oven. Let the shortcakes cool before serving them.

STRAWBERRY SHORTCAKE

SERVES 4

It is hard to go wrong with this dessert!

2 PINTS (OR 1 QUART OR 4 CUPS) STRAWBERRIES

1/3 CUP SUGAR

1 CUP WHIPPING CREAM

3 TABLESPOONS SUGAR

4 SHORTCAKES (SEE PRECEDING RECIPE)

EQUIPMENT LIST

STRAINER

CUTTING BOARD

PARING KNIFE OR 8-INCH
    SERRATED KNIFE

SMALL BOWL

MEASURING CUPS

FORK

SMALL, DEEP BOWL OR 4-CUP
    GLASS MEASURING CUP

MEASURING SPOONS

ROTARY BEATER

SPOON

4 DESSERT PLATES

1. Put the strawberries in a strainer and wash them under cold water. Shake the strainer to get rid of excess water. Spread the strawberries out on a board.

2. Cut the stems off the berries and set aside 4 of the nicest strawberries to decorate the top of each shortcake just before serving. Then slice the rest of the berries in

half. Put the strawberry slices in a bowl and sprinkle them with 1/3 cup sugar. With a fork, mash the berries until they are juicy. Set aside.

3. Put the whipping cream into a small, deep bowl; a 4-cup glass measuring cup is dandy. Add the 3 tablespoons sugar. Lower the rotary beater into the cream, letting it rest on the bottom of the bowl, and start whipping the cream by turning the handle rapidly. ("Whipping" means using a beater or a whisk to beat air into eggs or cream to make them grow larger in size and lighter.) At first, it seems that nothing is happening. But after a while, the cream starts thickening. You want to let it get

just thick or stiff enough so that when you lift the beater, the cream as it falls back into the bowl forms little mounds that don't sink and disappear. In cookbooks this is called whipping the cream until it makes soft peaks. Cover the bowl with plastic wrap and refrigerate if you're not using it right away.

4. Split the shortcakes in half and put the bottom halves on 4 dessert plates. Spoon about 1/3 cup of the berries and their juice over each shortcake. Now scoop up 3 or 4 big spoonfuls of whipped cream and spread it over the berries on each serving. Place the top half of the shortcake on each serving. Then put the remaining strawberries on top, dividing them evenly. Spoon 2 to 3 big spoonfuls of whipped cream onto the top and around the bottom of each shortcake and place a whole strawberry on top of each one. Serve right away.

Chapter 8

VEGETABLES

WHAT YOU WILL LEARN ABOUT

VEGETABLES

1. HOW TO BAKE A POTATO AND TEST IT FOR DONENESS.

2. HOW TO USE HERBS.

3. HOW TO BOIL CARROTS.

4. HOW TO PREPARE AND STEAM BROCCOLI.

5. HOW TO SAUTÉ ZUCCHINI.

Vegetables can be your good friends. They're easy to cook and the ones in this chapter are available all year round. Some vegetables, like a big baked potato with trimmings, can make a whole meal; usually, however, vegetables go along with the main course of a meal.

BAKED POTATOES

You will never starve if you know how to bake a potato. Once you learn how, you will be rewarded with the most satisfying food. Although I have never done it, I have often thought it might be fun to give a baked potato party. There are so many good things you can mash into a baked potato: salsa, grated cheese, sliced green onions, chopped tomatoes, crumbled bacon—the list goes on and on. For the party, you could lay out bowls with different fillings on the table along with a tray of hot baked potatoes, and add some refreshing drinks and fruit with cookies for dessert.

The potatoes people usually bake are the big ones called russet (or Idaho) potatoes. You can bake as many as you want at one time, as long as your oven is large enough to allow space for them to bake without touching one another. Here's how to do it for two people.

2 BAKING POTATOES

TO GO WITH THE POTATOES:

    BUTTER OR SOUR CREAM

    SALT AND PEPPER

1. Turn the oven on to 450° F. Make sure the rack is in the center of the oven.

EQUIPMENT LIST

VEGETABLE BRUSH

FORK

KITCHEN TIMER

**PARING KNIFE OR 8-INCH
    SERRATED KNIFE**

POT HOLDER

2. Scrub the potatoes with a brush under running water to remove all dirt.

3. Poke each potato with a fork to make 4 tiny holes so that the steam can escape through the holes when the potato gets hot as it bakes. If you don't make the holes, the steam sometimes causes the potato to explode in the oven. It is not only messy to clean up, but you lose the potato too.

4. Place them on the middle oven rack, slightly apart from one another.

5. Set the kitchen timer: Baking takes 1 hour for large potatoes, 50 minutes for medium potatoes, 45 minutes for small potatoes.

6. Test the potatoes for doneness by piercing a potato deep into the center with the tip of a paring knife to feel if it is soft and tender. You learn to tell the difference between a raw and a completely baked potato by testing with the paring knife 20 minutes after you put the potatoes in the oven. You will notice how hard they are at this point and how soft they will feel after the right amount of baking time. Try squeezing them with a pot holder near the end of the baking time, and you'll feel their softness.

7. Using a pot holder, remove the potatoes from the oven. Put them on a plate and break them open by poking a fork into each potato 2 or 3 times lengthwise. Squeeze them so they open wider. At this point you may want to put some butter or sour cream on the white insides and season them with a little salt and pepper. You can sprinkle on other toppings at this point. Eat them while they are hot.

A WORD ABOUT HERBS

Herbs have many purposes: All of them make gardens beautiful; some of them are good medicine; and many of them are used in cooking, both fresh and dried, to make food taste more flavorful. Using herbs can give a little drama to mild-tasting vegetables such as zucchini. You will learn a good cooking lesson when you taste the parsley and mint in the carrots and the thyme (pronounced "time") in the zucchini. Later, in the pasta lesson, you will use parsley, a fresh herb called basil, and dried bay leaves. And when you make the chicken dinner you will encounter another herb, called sage (see pages 149–51).

As you understand more and more about cooking you will probably become fascinated with trying different herbs with different foods. The most important point to remember about dried herbs is to taste them before you add them to a dish. Dried herbs can become old and dull, so you need to smell and taste them first and be sure to add enough to give flavor.

Parsley is the most popular herb of all. It is almost always used fresh. Bright green with tiny ruffled leaves, it tastes so mild and fresh that it is added to many dishes, often because it makes the food look pretty.

You might have thought mint was found only in chewing gum, but it is a lot more important than that. Mint is an herb that has been used and loved for centuries. It makes a fine cup of tea, it helps settle upset stomachs, and it gives a refreshing, lively flavor to lamb and to peas. See how you like it with carrots.

PARSLEY

BASIL

MINT

THYME

BOILED CARROTS WITH PARSLEY AND MINT

SERVES 3 OR 4

When I was growing up, everyone in my neighborhood cooked the same way. We had only three ways of cooking carrots: boiled and served salted with butter and parsley; roasted around meat, together with potatoes and onions, for special dinners; and my favorite, grated raw carrots with pineapple pieces for a salad. And of course we children ate lots of whole carrots raw, like rabbits. That's what my father called carrots—"rabbit food." Even picky eaters will munch raw carrots rabbit-style, and you don't need a recipe for raw carrots!

I've added fresh mint to this classic recipe—and there is a lesson on chopping herbs.

2 CUPS WATER

1/2 TEASPOON SALT

7 MEDIUM-SIZED CARROTS (ABOUT 1 POUND)

3 OR 4 SPRIGS PARSLEY

1 OR 2 SPRIGS FRESH MINT

2 TABLESPOONS BUTTER

1/4 TEASPOON SALT

EQUIPMENT LIST

MEASURING CUP

2-QUART SAUCEPAN

MEASURING SPOONS

PARING KNIFE OR 8-INCH
    SERRATED KNIFE

VEGETABLE PEELER

CUTTING BOARD

CHOPPING KNIFE

BOWL

SCISSORS

LARGE SPOON

KITCHEN TIMER

SLOTTED SPOON

1. Put 2 cups water in a 2-quart pan and put it on the stove. Turn the heat on high and add the 1/2 teaspoon salt.

2. Trim the coarse tops and the root tips off the carrots. Peel them with a vegetable peeler. Slice or snap the carrots in half, then cut them crosswise into rounds about 1/4 inch thick. If you want to try slicing with a big knife, try slicing 2 carrots at a time: Place 2 carrots side by side, with the thick, bottom end of 1 carrot next to the thin end of the other carrot. Take the chopping knife (also called a "chef's knife") and cut the pieces from them both at the same time, remembering to keep your fingertips tucked under. Put the pieces of carrot into a bowl and place the bowl near the stove.

3. Remove and discard the stems from the parsley and mint sprigs. With a chef's knife, chop the leaves into tiny pieces, or snip them with scissors. Set aside.

4. When the water begins to boil, use a large spoon to carefully slide the carrots into the boiling water, leaving the bowl alongside the stove.

5. Set the kitchen timer for 8 minutes, although it usually takes carrots about 10 to 12 minutes to cook.

6. Test the doneness of the carrots after 8 minutes by removing a slice or two of carrot with a large spoon. Let them cool a minute and take a bite: If they are tender they are done. Otherwise, cook them for a few more minutes.

7. Turn off the heat. Take a long-handled spoon with holes in it (a slotted spoon) or a pasta server and carefully scoop the carrots out of the pan, letting the water drain away, and put them into the bowl.

8. Add the chopped parsley, mint, and 2 tablespoons butter. Gently toss the carrots with a large spoon, so the butter melts and the carrots are evenly coated with the herbs and butter. Now add the 1/4 teaspoon salt, and gently stir the carrots again. Serve.

CHOPPING HERBS

You almost always chop fresh herbs when you are using them in cooking, unless you want just a sprig as decoration to make a plate look pretty.

Instead of chopping with a knife you can use a pair of scissors to snip leaves into tiny pieces; but chopping (and slicing) with a big knife initiates you to a whole new world—when you're ready.

When you graduate to chopping with a knife, use a big one for herbs—as big as 12 inches long. It may look dangerous, but if you handle a knife correctly the way a chef does, it is a safe and efficient tool. On your chopping board make a little bundle of the leaves of herbs and holding the knife in one hand by the handle, with the fingers of your other hand resting on the tip of the blade, start chopping by rocking the handle up and down. Now move the knife a little and continue, gradually moving the blade across the pile of leaves until all the leaves are finely chopped. This "rock-chop" method is rhythmic and fun to do.

When you need to clean off the chef's knife, wipe it carefully with a paper towel, not your fingers. The blade is sharp!

STEAMED BROCCOLI WITH GARLIC AND OLIVE OIL

EQUIPMENT LIST

STEAMER BASKET

4-QUART SAUCEPAN WITH LID

PARING KNIFE OR 8-INCH
    SERRATED KNIFE

KITCHEN TIMER

MEASURING SPOONS

CUTTING BOARD

SMALL SKILLET

SPOON

POT HOLDER

FORK OR TONGS

LARGE SPOON

SERVING BOWL

You'd never think, looking at it, that broccoli is a member of the cabbage family. It certainly doesn't look like a head of cabbage, but they are relatives. Adventurous Italians who wanted to start a new life in America came here bringing broccoli seeds with them. They knew they would miss the tastes of home, and broccoli was a food they loved in the old country, so it would be comforting to have here when they were homesick. Soon most of America was happily eating broccoli.

Steaming broccoli is a good method of cooking it because the broccoli keeps its fine texture and taste, but steaming too long makes broccoli lose its bright green color. So take a peek once or twice while it's steaming, and when it looks as though the color is fading, take it off the heat. It will still be a little crunchy, and it is very good with the olive oil and garlic sauce. Broccoli needs to be salted more than many vegetables. Taste and salt until you think it is right.

1 BUNCH BROCCOLI (ABOUT 1 POUND)

2 TABLESPOONS OLIVE OIL

1 TABLESPOON COLD WATER

1 LARGE CLOVE GARLIC

1/2 TEASPOON SALT

1. Put a steamer basket into a 4-quart or larger saucepan. Fill the pan with enough water so that it is just below the bottom of the steamer basket. Have a lid for the saucepan nearby.

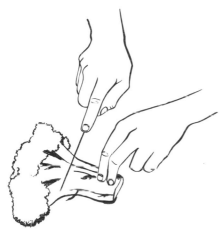

2. Cut the little bouquets of broccoli off the large, thick stems or snap them off with your fingers. Discard the thick stems. Now you have the broccoli flowerets, which look like tiny trees. Separate the tiny tree trunks with their green bushy tops. When they are all separated, place them in the steamer basket and put the lid on. Turn the heat to medium-high. Set the kitchen timer for 6 minutes.

3. While the broccoli is cooking, pour the olive oil and water into a small bowl. Put the clove of garlic on a board and give it a whack with the flat bottom of a skillet to smash it a little and loosen the peel. Then peel it and chop it into very tiny pieces. Stir it into the olive oil and water with a spoon. The olive oil and water separate easily, but don't worry about it.

4. Test the broccoli for doneness when the kitchen timer rings. Use a pot holder and slide the pan off the burner. Remove the lid carefully, tilting the lid away from you and keeping your face away from the hot steam. Use a fork or tongs, and take a piece of broccoli, pierce it, and if it is tender, it is done. If it is still too hard or too firm, put the lid back on, slide the pan back over the burner, and steam for 2 or 3 more minutes.

5. Put a serving bowl near the pan, and use a large spoon or tongs to transfer the broccoli pieces to the bowl. Sprinkle the 1/2 teaspoon salt over the broccoli, then give a stir to the water, olive oil, and garlic and add to the broccoli. Use a large spoon to toss and mix everything well. Serve hot or cold.

SAUTÉED ZUCCHINI WITH HERB BUTTER

SERVES 2 OR 3 (MAKES ABOUT 2 CUPS)

Zucchini is a very agreeable vegetable; it gets along with any food it's introduced to. Here we are going to sauté the zucchini—a quick way of cooking it. "Sauté" means to cook rapidly in a skillet with a little fat like butter or oil. You have to stay by the stove while you sauté, and you need to keep the food moving. It helps to shake the pan while you're stirring so the chunks of zucchini keep jumping and turning around on all sides. (The word "sauté" means "jump" in French.) The cooking will take only about 5 minutes.

3 ZUCCHINI

2 TABLESPOONS BUTTER

1/2 TEASPOON DRIED THYME LEAVES

1/4 TEASPOON SALT

1 PINCH PEPPER (A PINCH IS THE AMOUNT YOU CAN HOLD BETWEEN YOUR THUMB AND FORE-FINGER. BUT DON'T BE STINGY WHEN YOU PINCH!)

EQUIPMENT LIST

CUTTING BOARD

PARING KNIFE OR 8-INCH SERRATED KNIFE

MEDIUM-SIZED SKILLET

MEASURING SPOONS

LONG-HANDLED SPOON

KITCHEN TIMER

FORK

1. Wash the zucchini under cold water. Line them up side by side on a cutting board, touching one another. With a paring knife cut off all the stem tops and the round, brown ends of the zucchini and discard them. Cut each zucchini first in half, then slice each half lengthwise, from top to bottom, so each zucchini is now cut into 4 long pieces. Bunch the 4 pieces together and slice them crosswise into chunks about 1/2 inch thick, about as thick as a slice of bread.

2. Put a medium-sized skillet on a burner. Put the 2 tablespoons butter in the skillet and turn the heat to medium-low. As the butter melts and starts to bubble, put the 1/2 teaspoon thyme in the palm of one hand; holding both hands over the skillet, rub them together to crumble the thyme, letting it fall into the skillet. (Rubbing herbs between your warm palms crumbles them finer and releases more flavor.) Stir the butter and thyme together.

3. Add the zucchini chunks to the skillet and stir them around with a long-handled spoon to coat them with the butter mixture. Keep the zucchini spread in the pan in a single layer. This allows all the zucchini to get the same amount of heat so it will all cook in the same amount of time. Sprinkle with 1/4 teaspoon salt and a pinch of pepper. Set the timer for 5 minutes.

4. While the zucchini is cooking, keep stirring it around with the long-handled spoon. Hold the skillet handle in your other hand, shaking it quickly back and forth as you stir. When the timer bell rings, slide the skillet off the stove burner. Spear a zucchini chunk with a fork. Blow on it to cool it off a little and bite into it to check for doneness. It will still be a little firm, but remember it is still cooking while it is hot and will keep getting softer for a minute or so; by the time it gets to the table it will be nicely tender. If it is still quite hard and raw, put the skillet over the heat again and let the zucchini cook 2 more minutes. Serve hot or cold.

ABOUT THYME

There is an old cook's saying that goes, "When in doubt add thyme to whatever you're cooking." This means that the flavor of thyme pleases most people and mixes well with most foods. See if you agree.

Chapter 9

PASTA

1. ABOUT TOMATOES—THAT THEY CAN BE DRESSED DIFFERENTLY IN THE SUMMER AND IN THE WINTER, JUST LIKE YOU.

2. HOW TO MAKE A SUMMER TOMATO SAUCE OF FRESH TOMATOES, ONIONS, GARLIC, AND BASIL.

3. HOW TO MAKE A WINTER TOMATO SAUCE THAT IS RICH, CREAMY, AND SMOOTH.

4. HOW TO COOK SPAGHETTI.

5. HOW TO SAUCE THE SPAGHETTI.

6. HOW TO MAKE A BASIC WHITE SAUCE, WHICH WILL REVEAL THE MYSTERIES OF THICKENING.

7. HOW TO COOK MACARONI.

One of my earliest childhood memories is of our kitchen, where there was always a saucepan of tomato sauce bubbling on the back of the stove. There was also a large, striped can of olive oil sitting by the back

door, and a row of garlic heads on the
windowsill. This was an Italian kitchen,
and it was the room my grandmother lived in. She felt at home sitting
at the kitchen table, stringing green beans, shelling peas, chopping
garlic, or knitting heavy wool socks for my father while she waited
until it was time to begin preparing another meal.

Her cure for sadness, bruises, or hunger pangs was a piece of bread
spread with olive oil or a little of the bubbling tomato sauce. She believed that this simple cure would always cheer you up. When you
learn how to make the winter tomato sauce and the summer tomato
sauce recipes here, not only will you have something good to put on
pasta, string beans, zucchini, hot rice, and pizza, but you may also have
a cure for some of those troubled moments in life.

The next pasta dish you will do, macaroni and cheese, is one of
America's most beloved baked dishes. It is made with a cream sauce,
which is a basic flour, butter, and milk sauce that can be used for all
sorts of different dishes—baked vegetables, for example, such as potatoes or cauliflower.

SUMMER TOMATO SAUCE

MAKES 1 1/2 CUPS
(ENOUGH FOR 5 OR 6 CUPS COOKED PASTA)

If you plan to cook the spaghetti and make this sauce in order to eat it right away, read the spaghetti directions on pages 99–101. Start the spaghetti first, and while you are waiting for the water to boil, begin making the sauce. The spaghetti cooking and the sauce making should both be finished at about the same time. Then all you will have to do is toss the sauce and spaghetti together, serve it on plates or in bowls, sit down, take a deep breath, and eat.

EQUIPMENT LIST

CUTTING BOARD

SMALL SKILLET

MEASURING SPOONS

CHOPPING KNIFE

LARGE MIXING BOWL

PARING KNIFE OR 8-INCH
SERRATED KNIFE

1 LARGE CLOVE GARLIC

1/4 TEASPOON SALT

2 GREEN ONIONS (SCALLIONS)*

2 LARGE RIPE TOMATOES, OR 5 OR 6 SMALL ROMA

TOMATOES

4 SPRIGS PARSLEY

6 FRESH BASIL LEAVES

3 TABLESPOONS OLIVE OIL

*In the west, we call scallions "green onions." In the east, we call green onions "scallions." But all you have to remember is that scallions and green onions are long, skinny vegetables with long, green floppy tops and little white bulbs with roots on the bottom—and they are good to eat raw.

1. Put the clove of garlic on a cutting board and give it a whack with the bottom of a small skillet. You'll see that smashing it loosens the outer peel of the garlic clove so that you can now easily take it off and discard it. Sprinkle the 1/4 teaspoon salt over the garlic and chop the garlic into tiny pieces. The salt captures some of the garlic juices, which adds to the flavor of your sauce. Put the garlic and salt into a large mixing bowl.

2. Cut about 2 inches off from the coarse tops of the 2 green onions and discard them. Cut away any little roots on the bottom white part. Put the green onions side by side and slice them crosswise into small pieces. Add them to the garlic in the bowl.

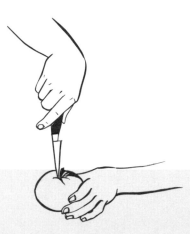

3. With the point of a small paring knife, cut the small round stem end of the tomatoes and pry out the core. Discard it.

4. Cut the tomatoes in half from top to bottom, and put them cut side down on a cutting board. Cut each half crosswise into 4 or 5 slices. Turn the slices flat on the board and cut them into small pieces. Add them to the bowl.

5. Bunch the 4 sprigs of parsley together and chop them into small pieces. Stack the 6 basil leaves, one on top of the other, and cut them lengthwise into about 3 or 4 strips, then turn them and cut into small pieces. Add the parsley and the basil to the bowl.

6. Now add the 3 tablespoons olive oil to the bowl and toss everything together gently, using your clean hands or a large spoon. Taste; if more salt is needed, sprinkle a little over the top of all the ingredients. Toss to mix the salt all around. If you are going to use this sauce later, cover the bowl with plastic wrap and refrigerate until needed.

WINTER TOMATO SAUCE

MAKES 1 1/2 CUPS
(ENOUGH FOR 5 OR 6 CUPS COOKED PASTA)

1 SMALLISH ONION

16-OUNCE CAN WHOLE PEELED TOMATOES

2 TABLESPOONS OLIVE OIL

1/4 CUP WATER

1/2 TEASPOON SUGAR

1 BAY LEAF

2 TABLESPOONS BUTTER

EQUIPMENT LIST

PARING KNIFE OR 8-INCH
SERRATED KNIFE

CUTTING BOARD

SMALL BOWL

CAN OPENER

MEDIUM-SIZED BOWL

MEDIUM-SIZED SAUCEPAN

MEASURING SPOONS

LONG-HANDLED SPOON

MEASURING CUP

KITCHEN TIMER

1. Cut the papery pointed stem end off the onion and cut off the fuzzy brown roots. Peel off the papery outer skin. Cut the onion in half, from the stem top to the bottom. Put each half cut side down on a cutting board and slice each half crosswise into 7 or 8 slices. Now cut the slices the other way 4 or 5 times to make lots of little pieces. Put the chopped onion into a small bowl and set it near the stove.

2. Open the can of tomatoes and pour the tomatoes and their juice into a medium-sized bowl. Wash your hands and use them to squish the tomatoes, pulling and shredding all the big chunks of tomato into little pieces.

3. Put a medium-sized saucepan on a stove burner and turn the heat to medium-high. Pour the 2 tablespoons olive oil into the pan, and tilt and turn it a little so the oil runs over the bottom and covers it.

4. After a few seconds check to see if the saucepan is hot by holding your hand an inch or two above the bottom. If it feels warm, add the onions. Stir them around with a long-handled spoon so they get coated with the olive oil. You want to cook the onions just long enough to soften them and get rid of their crisp rawness. Stay by the pan, holding the handle firmly in one hand and stirring with the other every few seconds. The onions will be cooked enough after 2 or 3 minutes, when they will feel softer as your spoon touches them.

5. Pour the tomatoes and tomato juice into the saucepan, then the 1/4 cup water. Stir to mix the onion, tomatoes, and water. Add 1/2 teaspoon sugar. Break the bay leaf in half and add it to the sauce. Stir again to mix the sauce well.

6. Set the kitchen timer for 15 minutes, but stay in the kitchen and stir the sauce every couple of minutes. If the sauce begins to boil rapidly, lower the heat to medium-low or low. This sauce should simmer, with just a few bubbles breaking on top.

7. When the timer rings, add the 2 tablespoons butter and stir the sauce a few seconds until the butter has melted into it. Remove the pan from the stove. Use a spoon to capture the 2 pieces of bay leaf and throw them away. If you aren't going to use the sauce right away, let it cool, then put it in a jar with a lid and store in the refrigerator until needed.

SPAGHETTI

SERVES 2 TO 3 (MAKES 5 OR 6 CUPS COOKED SPAGHETTI)

2 QUARTS COLD WATER

1 1/2 TEASPOONS SALT

1/2 POUND SPAGHETTI

1. Put a large pot on a stove burner. (The pot has to be big enough so that the water only half fills it.) Pour 2 quarts (8 cups) of cold water into the pot and add 1 1/2 teaspoons salt.

2. Turn the heat on high and let the water heat up until it starts to boil. When the water has begun to bubble all over the top it is time to add the spaghetti.

3. Drop the spaghetti into the water (or into the pasta strainer inserted into the boiling water—see page 101) and use a long-handled fork or a pasta server to push any spaghetti sticking above the water down into the pot so that all the strands are covered with boiling water. (A pasta server is a long-handled tool with an end that looks like a claw with holes in it.) Use the pasta server or the fork to stir and separate the strands of spaghetti so that they don't stick together in clumps. When the water comes to a boil again, set a kitchen

EQUIPMENT LIST

LARGE POT

MEASURING CUP

MEASURING SPOONS

PASTA SERVER OR LONG-HANDLED FORK

KITCHEN TIMER

LARGE BOWL

STEP STOOL

LONG-HANDLED SPOON

PASTA OR SOUP BOWLS

timer for 12 minutes. Don't cover the pot. Stir the pot again just to be sure the spaghetti is moving freely around in the water.

4. When the kitchen timer rings, take the pasta server again and fish out a strand or two of spaghetti with it. Lift it out of the water, give it a few seconds to cool (or run it under the cold water faucet), and take a bite. If it is tender and not hard, it is done. If it is still hard, let the spaghetti cook another 2 to 3 minutes. Turn off the heat.

5. Set a large bowl next to the pot. Now, to get the spaghetti out of the pot, dip the pasta server into the water and capture some spaghetti on it. You may have to stand on a short stool for this operation. Lift it out, hold it above the pot for a couple of seconds to let the water drip off, then turn the pasta server upside-down over the bowl to plop the spaghetti into it. Repeat until you have removed all the spaghetti to the bowl.

If you don't have a pasta server, use a long-handled fork: Hold it upright, touching the bottom of the pan, and twist it around and around to wrap the spaghetti around it. Lift it above the pot to drain and drop the spaghetti into the bowl.

If you have used a pasta strainer, pull the strainer out of the water.

6. Serve the spaghetti hot, tossed and mixed with either summer or winter tomato sauce. For spaghetti with summer tomato sauce, toss the cool sauce together with the hot pasta using the pasta server or a long-handled fork and a big spoon, and serve in individual bowls. For spaghetti with winter tomato sauce, have the sauce bubbling hot (reheat if necessary), and pour it over the pasta. Toss it so all the strands are covered with sauce and serve in individual bowls.

THE HANDY PASTA STRAINER

One of the toughest jobs for young and old people alike is lifting a big pot full of boiling water from the stove and draining the contents into a strainer or colander in the sink.

I've recommended ways of fishing pasta out of the water, but the ideal solution is to cook the pasta in a deep strainer called a pasta strainer, which is lowered into boiling water. Then you have only to pull the strainer out by the handle, letting the water run back into the pot, which solves the whole problem. Vegetables and rice cooked in boiling water can be handled in the same way.

MACARONI AND CHEESE

Macaroni and cheese is a dish your grandmother made and your parents probably make, but now it's your turn! Macaroni and cheese is great all by itself, but it's even better with a green salad like the one in Chapter 2.

EQUIPMENT LIST

- 1 1/2- TO 2-QUART (6 TO 8 CUPS) OVENPROOF CASSEROLE OR BAKING DISH
- LARGE SAUCEPAN
- MEASURING CUPS
- MEASURING SPOONS
- LONG-HANDLED FORK OR SPOON, OR A PASTA SERVER
- WAXED PAPER
- CHEESE GRATER
- KITCHEN TIMER
- SMALL SAUCEPAN
- LARGE WOODEN SPOON
- LONG-HANDLED SLOTTED SPOON
- STEP STOOL
- COLANDER OR LARGE STRAINER
- POT HOLDERS

2 QUARTS (8 CUPS) WATER

1 TEASPOON SALT

1 1/2 CUPS SMALL ELBOW MACARONI

1/2-POUND CHUNK SHARP CHEDDAR CHEESE

   (ABOUT 1 CUP GRATED)

2 TABLESPOONS BUTTER

4 TEASPOONS FLOUR

1 CUP MILK

SALT AND PEPPER

1. Turn the oven on to 350° F. Make sure the rack is in the center of the oven. Get out a medium-sized casserole or baking dish to put the macaroni in when it's time to bake it.

2. Put a large saucepan on a stove burner and pour 2 quarts water into it. Add 1 teaspoon salt and turn the heat to high. (Insert a pasta basket if you are using one—see box, page 101.)

3. Measure out 1 1/2 cups macaroni and set by the stove. Put a long-handled fork or spoon or a pasta server close by.

4. While you're waiting for the water to boil, spread a piece of waxed paper about the size of a paper towel on the counter. Set a grater on top of the waxed paper and grate the chunk of cheddar cheese onto it. You need to grate an amount of cheese about the size of 2 sticks of butter to make about 1 cup grated cheese.

5. When the water is boiling, slowly add the macaroni and stir it with the long-handled fork or spoon. Stir 2 or 3 times during the first few minutes so the macaroni doesn't stick to the bottom of the pan.

6. Set the timer for 12 minutes. While the macaroni is cooking, put the 2 tablespoons butter into a small saucepan and turn the heat to medium. It only takes a minute to melt butter, so stand right by the stove. When the butter has melted, tip and tilt the saucepan so the butter covers the bottom of the pan.

7. Sprinkle 4 teaspoons flour over the butter and stir the flour and butter together with a large wooden spoon, getting all over the bottom of the saucepan with your spoon. When the flour is added to the butter, the mixture will foam up and become a thick mass of bubbles. Do a really good job of mixing and blending and hold the handle of the saucepan the whole time. Don't relax! It is important to keep stirring all the time as the butter and flour cook for about 2 minutes.

8. Slide the saucepan off the burner, and let the butter and flour mixture rest until the bubbling stops. Slide the saucepan back onto the burner, and add the milk. Keep stirring vigorously. You have to stir *all* the sauce—not just one little spot, but all around the bottom and sides of the saucepan. You want the sauce to become smooth and creamy, so continue the stirring for a few minutes until the flour, butter, and milk mixture thickens. If the sauce begins to boil, turn the heat down very low. Continue stirring for several minutes. When the sauce has thickened a little and is smooth, turn off the heat and slide the pan off the burner again.

9. Pick up the piece of waxed paper by two corners and dump half the grated cheese into the hot sauce. Stir until the cheese has melted and the sauce is smooth, creamy, and all yellow. Taste it—if it seems a little bland, lightly salt and pepper it. (Cheese is often salty, so it may be just right without extra salt.)

10. When the timer rings, using a large spoon or pasta server, fish a piece of macaroni out of the water. Blow on it to cool it a bit and take a bite. If it is tender and not firm and rubbery, it is cooked. If it is not tender, cook another 2 or 3 minutes. When the macaroni is cooked, turn off the heat under the pot.

11. To get the macaroni out of the hot water, either scoop them out with a slotted spoon or pasta server or drain the pot in the sink. (Or lift out the pasta strainer. See box, page 101)

To scoop them out, first have the casserole ready by the stove to put the macaroni into. Then remove the macaroni from the water with a long-handled slotted spoon or pasta server. You may need a short stool to stand on while you are doing this. Scoop the macaroni out of the pot, a spoonful at a time, and hold the spoon above the pot for a few seconds to drain off the water; then drop the macaroni into the casserole.

The second way depends on how tall and strong you are and how confident you feel about carrying a pan of hot water to the sink. Set a colander or large strainer in the sink. If you can lift the saucepan easily while holding it away from you, carry it to the sink and pour the water and macaroni into the colander or strainer so the water goes down the drain and the macaroni stays in the container. Put the drained macaroni into the casserole.

12. Pour the cheese sauce over the macaroni, and stir thoroughly until all the macaroni is coated with it. Now sprinkle the remaining 1/2 cup cheese all over the top.

13. Put the casserole, uncovered, into the oven. Set the kitchen timer for 30 minutes. Right now is a good time to wash the pots and pans you've used and to set the table.

14. When the timer rings, use pot holders to remove the casserole from the oven. Take a spoon and insert it down to the bottom of the casserole, and take out a couple pieces of the macaroni. Taste them carefully to make sure they're hot. If the macaroni doesn't seem hot enough set the kitchen timer for 10 more minutes, and put the casserole back in the oven. Serve the macaroni and cheese hot: The dish doesn't taste good cold.

Chapter 10

BREAD and PIZZA

1. EVERYTHING YOU NEED TO KNOW ABOUT YEAST AND HOW IT WORKS.

2. HOW TO MIX AND KNEAD A BREAD DOUGH.

3. HOW TO LET THE DOUGH RISE AND HOW TO PUNCH IT DOWN AGAIN.

4. HOW TO FORM AND BAKE A LOAF.

5. HOW TO SHAPE A SMALL PIZZA.

6. HOW TO BAKE AND TOP THE PIZZA.

In this lesson you will make one kind of dough that can be used for bread or pizza. You can make one small loaf of bread and an 8-inch pizza, as called for here, or you can make two little loaves of bread with the dough and skip the pizza, or you can make two pizzas and skip the bread—whatever strikes your fancy.

Today everybody knows what a pizza is, but Italian housewives knew about it first. On baking day they would simply pinch off a little of the dough they had prepared for making bread and they would flatten the piece out and bake themselves a little pizza for lunch. And that's exactly what you're going to do.

YEAST

Yeast is different from any other ingredient that you use in cooking, because it is alive. The live yeast cells are too small to see, but when you make bread, you will see and feel how the yeast changes the bread dough. The dough grows bigger and bigger and becomes soft and puffy from the little air pockets the yeast creates. When you punch the air out of the dough, you get rid of all the air pockets, but the yeast will get busy and put them all back again. This is just what we want them to do, because that action is what makes our bread strong enough to hold together instead of crumbling apart, and light enough so that we can eat it without breaking our teeth. When you put your bread into the oven, the bread will grow, or rise higher. Then it slowly becomes set in the heat.

The yeast called for in this recipe is dried yeast, which needs to be brought back to life with some warm water and a pinch of sugar. Once it is activated, the yeast loves to live in bread dough. It feeds on the starch and sugar in the flour, and it thrives in warm temperatures. If you put yeast in cold water, it grows very slowly. If you put it in warm water, it grows quickly. The most important point to remember is that very hot liquid (over 120° F.) will kill yeast. When you're learning to make bread, it is a good idea to use liquid that is just warm enough for you to stick your finger in and hold it there comfortably.

BASIC DOUGH FOR BREAD AND PIZZA

ENOUGH DOUGH FOR ONE SMALL LOAF OF BREAD
AND ONE 8-INCH PIZZA

1/4 CUP WARM WATER

1/4-OUNCE PACKAGE (1 TABLESPOON) ACTIVE DRY
YEAST

A PINCH OF SUGAR (THE AMOUNT YOU CAN PINCH
BETWEEN YOUR THUMB AND FOREFINGER) FOR
FEEDING THE YEAST

1 TABLESPOON BUTTER

1 CUP MILK

2 TEASPOONS SUGAR

1 1/2 TEASPOONS SALT

APPROXIMATELY 3 CUPS ALL-PURPOSE FLOUR

VEGETABLE SHORTENING

EQUIPMENT LIST

MEASURING CUPS

LARGE MIXING BOWLS

MEASURING SPOONS

SMALL SAUCEPAN

LARGE SPOON

CUTTING BOARD

6- BY 3 1/2- BY 2-INCH BREAD
PAN

TOWEL

KITCHEN TIMER

POT HOLDERS

COOLING RACK

1. Pour 1/4 cup warm water into a large mixing bowl. Sprinkle 1/4 ounce yeast and the pinch of sugar over the water. Stir, and then let the mixture stand for 5 minutes until the yeast grains dissolve and the liquid looks smooth. As the yeast melts, some foamy islands will form on the surface, which mean the yeast is alive and growing.

2. Put 1 tablespoon butter in a small saucepan on a burner and turn the heat to low. When the butter has almost all melted add the milk and continue to heat until the butter is completely melted and the milk is warm. Take the pan off the stove and test the milk to make sure it isn't too hot for the yeast. Stick your finger quickly into the milk; if you can hold it there and the liquid feels just warm, that's fine, but if it feels very hot, let it cool for 5 minutes, and then add the milk–butter mixture to the yeast mixture.

3. Add the 2 teaspoons sugar, the 1 1/2 teaspoons salt, and 2 1/2 cups of the flour to the yeast and milk mixture. Save the remaining 1/2 cup flour for the next few steps. Stir well with a large spoon to mix together the liquid and dry ingredients. Sprinkle a little flour onto a cutting board. Scoop up the dough with your hands and gently press it into a ball. If it feels too sticky to handle, put it back in the bowl, add a little more flour, and work that into the dough by squeezing and patting. Don't worry about not mixing the flour in completely: Kneading will take care of that.

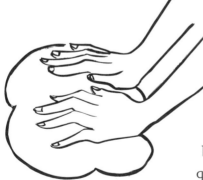

4. Put the ball of dough on the board. Sprinkle a little more flour on top of the dough and begin kneading it. Kneading dough gives it strength, so the air bubbles that the yeast create stay trapped inside the loaf and make the bread light. Press down on the dough with the heel of your palms, pushing it away from you. Fold the dough back toward yourself, give it a quarter-turn, and repeat. As you knead, add a sprinkle of flour when the dough becomes sticky, but don't add too much; use only as much as you need to keep the dough from sticking to your hands and the board.

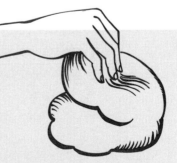

Below: Kneading the dough and cutting a finished loaf

Above: A seasoned young cook kneading the dough

Left: Rolling out the pie dough
Right: Serving a wedge of freshly baked apple pie

The dough will look and feel smooth and stretchy (a little like bubble gum after you've chewed it a while). It will feel springy and almost alive under your fingers. Keep kneading for 5 minutes. (Don't cheat on this step. The dough needs to be kneaded. In fact, you can't knead it too much.) Gather the dough into a ball. Then to test whether you have kneaded enough, poke the dough with your index finger, and if the dough springs back and the hole disappears, you've kneaded enough.

5. Grease a large mixing bowl with vegetable shortening and put your dough in it. Cover the bowl with plastic wrap. Now the dough will begin to rise. Let it rise until it is twice as big as its original size. (Some people say, "until it has doubled in bulk.") Depending on how warm your room is, the rising will take an hour or more. Be patient.

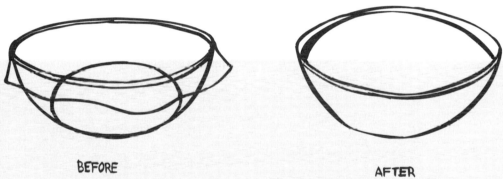

BEFORE   AFTER

6. Grease the inside of a 6- by 3 1/2- by 2-inch bread pan with vegetable shortening.

When the dough in the bowl is about twice as big as when you put it into the bowl, punch it down in several places. Punching knocks the air out of the dough.

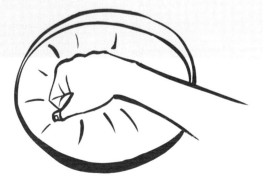

7. Spread a small handful of flour in a big circle on a board. Turn the dough out of the bowl onto the floured board and cut it in half. Half the dough is for the loaf of bread, and the other half is for a pizza. The bread dough needs to be shaped into a loaf, which then rises one more time in its pan. You can use the other half of the dough to make a pizza while the loaf of bread is rising again, or you can wrap the pizza dough in plastic, refrigerate it, and make a pizza later. (But use the dough within a day.)

Form the loaf of bread by patting the dough into a little football shape that will fit into the 6- by 3 1/2- by 2-inch bread pan. Put it into the pan and smooth the top with your hands to make it even. The dough should come halfway up the sides of the pan. If it looks lumpy or rough, pat it with your fingers to smooth it.

8. Cover the pan loosely with a towel and let the dough rise to the top of the pan or a little over. Depending on how warm or cold your room is, it will take this loaf anywhere from 30 to 60 minutes to rise that much. After 15 minutes turn your oven on to 350° F. so it will be ready to bake your bread. Set the rack in the middle of the oven.

9. When the dough has risen all the way to the top of the pan, you are ready to bake your bread. Remove the towel and check. (If you baked a pizza while the bread was rising, be sure to turn the oven down to 350° F.) Put the baking pan in the oven and set the timer for 35 minutes. After 35 minutes, check your bread. If it is golden brown on top, it is done. If not, bake another 5 to 10 minutes until it is.

10. When the loaf is done, use pot holders to remove the pan from the oven. Then turn the loaf out of the pan onto a rack and let it cool at least 10 minutes before you slice it.

PIZZA

You can make a little pizza whenever you make bread, or you can save a piece of the dough, wrap it in plastic wrap, refrigerate it, and bake a pizza the next day. (But don't keep the dough in the refrigerator longer than overnight.) By the way, the Italian word for a small pizza is *pizzetta*.

1/2 RECIPE FOR BREAD DOUGH (SEE PRECEDING RECIPE, PAGE 111)

1 TABLESPOON OLIVE OIL

VEGETABLE SHORTENING

1/2 ONION

ABOUT 1/2 CUP GRATED CHEDDAR CHEESE

1 TOMATO

ROLLING PIN

MEASURING SPOONS

BAKING SHEET

SPATULA

KITCHEN TIMER

PARING KNIFE OR 8-INCH SERRATED KNIFE

CHEESE GRATER

POT HOLDERS

1. Preheat the oven to 450° F.

2. Turn the dough out onto a floured work surface. With your hands, flatten and stretch the piece of bread dough into a circle about 8 or 9 inches across. Use your fingertips and the heels of your hands to push down and outwards. Don't worry: You can't hurt this dough. If you have to struggle because the dough is springy and won't hold its shape, use a rolling pin and that will flatten it out more quickly.

3. Pour 1 tablespoon olive oil in the middle of the circle. With your fingers, spread it all over the dough.

4. Grease a baking sheet with vegetable shortening. Put the baking sheet next to your pizza dough. Loosen the dough with a spatula if it is sticking to the surface a little, and

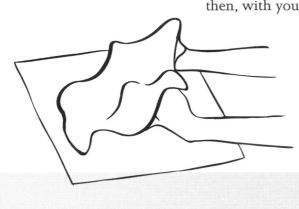

then, with your hands, carefully lift the dough and set it on the baking sheet. If it gets out of shape, pat it back into a circle with your hands. Turn the edges up a bit around the rim to make it neat, so it looks like a pizza.

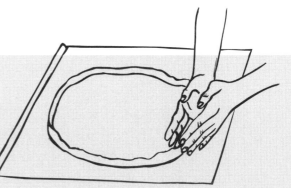

5. Put the baking sheet in the oven and set the timer for 10 minutes. After 10 minutes, check the edges of the pizza. If they are still pale, bake another 3 to 4 minutes. If they are golden, the pizza is done. It usually takes about 12 to 15 minutes to bake completely.

6. While the pizza is baking, chop half an onion (see illustration, page 123), grate enough cheese for 1/2 cup (see illustration, page 103), and cut the tomato into 6 thick slices.

7. Remove the baking sheet from the oven with pot holders and set it on the cool stove top. If the dough has puffed up just give it a quick smack (it's hot!) with your hand to flatten it before you put your toppings on. Put the tomato slices on the pizza, then sprinkle the onions and cheese evenly all over the top. Using pot holders, put the pizza back in the oven to bake for about 2 more minutes, just until the cheese melts. Remove the baking sheet from the oven with pot holders, cut the pizza in slices or in half, and eat it right away.

Chapter 11

SUPPER STEAK

WHAT YOU LEARN MAKING

SUPPER STEAK

1. **HOW TO PREPARE AND COOK MUSHROOMS.**

2. **HOW TO PREPARE WATERCRESS.**

3. **HOW TO PAN-FRY STEAKS AND TEST FOR DONENESS.**

4. **HOW TO HAVE ALL PARTS OF THE MEAL READY, TO PUT THEM TOGETHER, AND TO SERVE HOT.**

This is a neat, speedy supper dish to fix, a simple meal with everything sitting on top of one slice of bread: first watercress, next mushrooms and onions, and then the main attraction—steak. First you cook the vegetables and set them aside, ready and waiting, while you cook the steak. Then you put everything together—bread, salad, vegetables, and meat—and all you have to do is spread your napkin on your lap and begin eating.

Juggling two or three parts to a supper is a big part of learning to cook. After you've been cooking for a while, you will see that in preparing some meals you can take a long time and be lazy about getting them cooked. But sometimes when you want to cook a speedy meal like Supper Steak, you have to pay attention and work quickly. When you are making a snappy meal it is most important to read the recipe carefully *before* you start cooking, because you want to have all the ingredients ready and lined up so you can zip through each step at the right time.

SUPPER STEAK

SERVES 2

To make this recipe you need two thin steaks. Because most filet steaks are usually twice as thick as you need for this recipe, ask your butcher to cut one thick 6- to 8-ounce filet steak in half horizontally to make two thin steaks.

EQUIPMENT LIST

LARGE SKILLET

PARING KNIFE OR 8-INCH
   SERRATED KNIFE

CUTTING BOARD

3 SMALL BOWLS

STRAINER

LONG-HANDLED SPOON

LARGE PLATE

METAL SPATULA

POT HOLDER

MEASURING CUP

FORK

2 SERVING PLATES

4 TABLESPOONS BUTTER (1/2 STICK)

1 MEDIUM ONION

ABOUT 6 OUNCES FRESH MUSHROOMS (1 1/2 CUPS SLICED)

1 BUNCH WATERCRESS

SALT AND PEPPER

2 THIN, 3- TO 4-OUNCE FILET STEAKS (ABOUT 1/2 INCH THICK)

1/2 CUP WATER

2 SLICES FRESH WHITE BREAD

1. Turn the oven on to 200° F.

2. Put half the butter (2 tablespoons) into a large skillet. Set the skillet on the stove, but don't turn the heat on yet.

3. Cut off and throw away the root end and the pointy tip of the onion and cut the onion in half from the stem top down. Peel off the paper-like skin and throw it away. Place the onion cut side down on a cutting board. Holding the onion with your fingers tucked under, cut slices 1/8 inch thick (about the thickness of 2 pennies). Make about 6 to 8 slices, going from the tip to the root end with your knife. You will have slices that are half-moon shaped. Keep slicing until you've cut up the whole onion. Put the onion slices in a small bowl and set near the stove.

4. Mushrooms need to be wiped clean. Dampen a paper towel with water, squeeze it so you get rid of excess water, and then lightly rub it over each mushroom. Hold onto the stem of each mushroom, wiggle it, and then push gently on the cap so that the cap separates easily from the stem. Put the caps on the cutting board, rounded side up, and cut each of them into about 4 slices. Cut the stems in half crosswise. Put the caps and stems in another bowl and set aside next to the onion slices.

5. Now prepare the watercress. You will use only the tiny stems and leaves. Break off the large coarse stems and throw them away. Put the leaves and small stems in a strainer and run cold water over them. Shake the strainer to get all the water out. Wrap the watercress in 2 or 3 paper towels and gently pat it dry. Put the watercress in a small bowl and set aside.

6. Turn the heat on under the skillet to medium. Tilt the skillet as the butter melts so the bottom of the skillet gets covered with butter.

7. Put the sliced onions and mushrooms into the skillet, then salt and pepper them lightly. Using a long-handled spoon, stir and move the vegetables slowly around. Cook them until they have softened a little, about 3 or 4 minutes. The onions will look slightly yellow and the mushrooms will have turned a little brown. Turn off the heat and use the spoon to scoop the vegetables out of the skillet and onto a large plate. Put them in the oven to keep warm.

8. Add the remaining 2 tablespoons butter to the skillet and turn the heat to high. Wait for about 30 seconds, then hold your hand about 2 inches above the bottom of the skillet; if you can feel some heat, the steaks are ready to go into the skillet. The butter should be sizzling. Stand back a little as you put them in so you don't get spattered. Salt and pepper the steaks lightly on top and pan-fry them for about a minute. Use a spatula or a fork to turn the steaks over. Lightly salt and pepper them again, and pan-fry for another minute. Just 2 minutes should be about right, but you also can make a small cut in the outside rim of the steak, opening up the slit and looking at the color of the meat. If it is bright red, it will still be very rare and you may want to cook it a little more. If it is pink, it is medium-rare. If it is gray the steak is well done.

9. Remove the skillet from the burner and let it sit a few seconds. Use a pot holder to remove the plate of onions and mushrooms from the oven. Set the plate by the stove. Remove the steaks from the skillet and place them on the warm plate with the onions and mushrooms. Put 2 other plates near the stove to serve the steaks on, because it will only take a minute now to finish the cooking.

10. Set the skillet back on the stove over high heat and pour in the water. Let the water bubble and cook for a few seconds while you stir and scrape the bits of steak off the bottom of the pan in order to mix all the flavors of vegetables and meat juices together. Turn off the heat.

11. Spear each slice of bread with a fork and dunk the bread into the skillet juices for just for a second. Place a slice of bread on each serving plate.

12. Scatter a handful of watercress over each piece of bread, saving a few sprigs for the top. Divide the mushrooms and onions in half and pile half of them on the watercress on one slice of bread and the other half over the watercress on the other slice. Spoon any juices left in the skillet over the vegetables.

13. Put a steak on top of the vegetables. Press down gently just a little with a spatula so that the juices drizzle through all the ingredients. Arrange a few sprigs of watercress on top. Eat while everything is very warm.

COOKIES and BROWNIES

WHAT YOU LEARN MAKING
COOKIES and BROWNIES

1. HOW TO MIX, SHAPE, AND BAKE OATMEAL COOKIES.

2. HOW TO MELT CHOCOLATE AND MIX A BROWNIE BATTER.

3. HOW TO BAKE, COOL, AND CUT BROWNIE SQUARES.

SOME TIPS ABOUT BAKING COOKIES

• Always preheat the oven at least 10 minutes before you start baking.

• Always use a kitchen timer.

• Always check carefully for doneness 2 or 3 minutes before the recommended baking time is up. Cookies are done when their edges are lightly browned, but for thick cookies like the ones in this lesson, you should check the bottom, too. See individual recipes for specific methods of checking. Don't leave the oven door open for longer than a minute when you check or your oven will cool off too much.

Next to dogs, cookies can be your best
friend. They fill in the little chinks in the day when
one is hungry for something sweet and rewarding. Neat and tidy,
cookies can be eaten without plates or forks, or they can take a
walk with you and be eaten as you stroll.

CHEWY OATMEAL RAISIN COOKIES

Now you'll never have to skip breakfast. Instead of having to eat your oatmeal and raisins in a bowl, you can carry these cookies with you for a portable breakfast, any time you like.

EQUIPMENT LIST

2 COOKIE SHEETS

MEASURING CUPS

MEASURING SPOONS

2 LARGE MIXING BOWLS

LARGE SPOON

KITCHEN TIMER

POT HOLDERS

METAL SPATULA

COOLING RACKS

VEGETABLE SHORTENING

1 1/4 CUPS FLOUR, MEASURED BY SCOOPING FLOUR

INTO THE CUP AND LEVELING IT WITH A KNIFE

1/2 TEASPOON BAKING SODA

1/2 TEASPOON SALT

1 1/2 TEASPOONS CINNAMON

1/2 TEASPOON NUTMEG

1 1/2 CUPS UNCOOKED OATMEAL (NOT INSTANT)

1/2 CUP SUGAR

1/2 CUP LIGHT-BROWN SUGAR, PACKED FIRMLY IN

THE MEASURING CUP

1 CUP RAISINS

1/2 CUP VEGETABLE OIL

1 EGG

1/4 CUP MILK

1. Turn the oven on to 350° F. With your fingers or a piece of paper, scoop up a little vegetable shortening and smear it all over the 2 cookie sheets to coat them lightly with grease.

2. Put the 1 1/4 cups flour, 1/2 teaspoon baking soda, 1/2 teaspoon salt, 1 1/2 teaspoons cinnamon, and 1/2 teaspoon nutmeg in a large mixing bowl. Stir with a large spoon until well mixed.

3. Put the 1 1/2 cups oatmeal, 1/2 cup sugar, 1/2 cup brown sugar, 1 cup raisins, 1/2 cup oil, 1 egg, and 1/4 cup milk in another large mixing bowl. Stir with a large spoon until well mixed.

4. Add the flour mixture to the oatmeal mixture. Stir the two together, stirring carefully at first so the flour doesn't fly all around. This dough is a little stiff, so use some energy and stir until the dough has no streaks or lumps left in it (except for the raisins).

5. Fill a teaspoon super-full with cookie dough. Using your finger, push the dough out of the teaspoon onto one of the cookie sheets. Continue to spoon up dough and push it onto the cookie sheet, keeping the mounds of dough about 2 inches apart.

Wet your fingers and press each cookie down just a little—don't press them completely flat.

6. When you've filled one cookie sheet with about 15 mounds of dough, put the cookie sheet in the oven on the middle rack. Set the timer for 8 minutes. While the first cookies are baking, fill the second sheet. When the timer bell rings, check to see if the cookies are lightly browned. If not, let them bake 2 more minutes. When they are lightly browned on top, pull the cookie sheet out of the oven a little with pot holders and lift one cookie up with a metal spatula so you can see the bottom. If the bottom is lightly browned, the cookies are done. Don't bake them any longer or they will be dry. Remove the cookie sheet from the oven with pot holders and place it on top of the stove. Put the second cookie sheet in the oven, reset the timer for 8 minutes, and bake the cookies exactly the same way. After you have taken them out of the oven let them cool for 5 minutes, then carefully remove them with a metal spatula and place them a little apart—on baking racks, on waxed paper, or on a large platter. When they are completely cool, store them in a cookie jar or in a big can with an airtight lid.

CHOCOLATE BROWNIES

MAKES THIRTY 2-INCH BROWNIES

You're going to be very proud of these brownies. They're the best in the world, yet they are very simple to make. A chocolate brownie can be eaten the same way as a cookie or served on a plate, with some vanilla ice cream, which will make a splendid dessert.

VEGETABLE SHORTENING

4 SQUARES (4 OUNCES) UNSWEETENED

    CHOCOLATE

1/4 POUND PLUS 4 TABLESPOONS (1 1/2 STICKS)

    BUTTER

2 CUPS SUGAR

3 EGGS

2 TEASPOONS VANILLA

1 CUP FLOUR, MEASURED BY SCOOPING FLOUR

    INTO THE CUP AND LEVELING IT WITH A KNIFE

1/2 TEASPOON SALT

1 CUP CHOPPED WALNUTS

EQUIPMENT LIST

9- BY 13-INCH BAKING PAN

LARGE SAUCEPAN

LONG-HANDLED SPOON

MEASURING CUPS

SMALL BOWL

FORK

MEASURING SPOONS

RUBBER SPATULA

KITCHEN TIMER

POT HOLDERS

COOLING RACK

KNIFE

SMALL METAL SPATULA

1. Turn on the oven to 350° F. Make sure the oven rack is in the middle. With vegetable shortening, grease the bottom and sides of a 9- by 13-inch baking pan.

2. Put the 4 squares chocolate and 1 1/2 sticks butter into a large saucepan and set it on the stove. Turn the heat to low. Melt the chocolate and butter, stirring often and holding on to the handle with your other hand. Don't go away! Chocolate can burn quickly if you don't pay attention. When the chocolate and butter are melted, remove the pan from the heat.

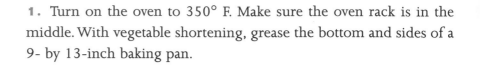

3. Add the 2 cups sugar to the chocolate and butter and stir until well blended.

4. Crack the 3 eggs into a small bowl and stir them around with a fork to break them up and blend them together. Add them to the chocolate mixture and stir well. Add the 2 teaspoons vanilla and stir again until the ingredients are completely blended and the mixture has no lumps or streaks.

5. Add the 1 cup flour, 1/2 teaspoon salt, and 1 cup chopped walnuts; stir until the batter is well mixed.

6. Pour the batter into the baking pan. With a rubber spatula spread it out evenly to the edges of the pan. Put the baking pan on the rack in the middle of the oven.

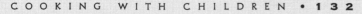

7. Set the timer for 20 minutes. When the timer rings, use a pot holder to pull the pan a little way out of the oven; insert a toothpick into the center of the brownies. If the toothpick comes out clean, with no sticky batter clinging to it, the brownies are done. They will probably need more baking after the first test—it usually takes 25 to 30 minutes to bake these, so try again after another 5 minutes.

8. Using pot holders, remove the brownies from the oven. Place the baking pan on a rack and let cool for 30 minutes. Cut the brownies into 2-inch squares, making 5 equally spaced cuts a little more than 2 inches apart on the long side of the pan and 4 cuts a little less than 2 inches apart on the short side. Remove the squares from the pan with a small metal spatula.

Chapter 13

WILLIE'S FRUIT CRISP and an APPLE PIE

FRUIT CRISP and an APPLE PIE

1. HOW TO PEEL AND SLICE APPLES.

2. HOW TO MAKE A CRISP TOPPING FOR A FRUIT CRISP.

3. HOW TO MIX PIE DOUGH AND ROLL IT OUT.

4. HOW TO LINE A PIE PLATE, FILL IT, ARRANGE THE TOP CRUST, AND SEAL IT.

5. HOW TO BAKE A PIE IN THE OVEN AND KNOW WHEN IT'S DONE.

Before you tackle the pie, first try
the fruit dessert known as a crisp. A crumbly top-
ping is sprinkled over fruit and the dessert is baked until the top is crisp and the
fruit soft. Each time you peel an apple you will get better at it. It takes a little practice to find your own comfortable way of holding the apple and the knife. A crisp
is simpler to make than a pie, and some people think it's just as good. You can use
the topping for all kinds of fruits and berries too.

The pie part of this lesson will teach you something most cooks never learn:
how to make a good flaky pie crust. It won't take you long to get the hang of it.
The key point to remember is the less you handle pie dough, the better it will be.
Read the directions and look at the illustrations carefully. Your hands are your best
tools for making pie dough. When you can make a good pie, you will have a special gift to give others that money can't buy.

WILLIE'S FRUIT CRISP

One young man I know calls this dessert Apple Heaven. It is best served warm. You can eat it plain, with heavy cream or whipped cream (see page 76 for detailed instructions), or with vanilla ice cream.

1/4 POUND (1 STICK) BUTTER, MELTED, PLUS A LIT-
TLE SOFT BUTTER FOR GREASING THE
BAKING DISH

6 LARGE FIRM APPLES (ABOUT 6 CUPS SLICED)

1 1/4 CUPS SUGAR

1 CUP PLUS 2 TABLESPOONS FLOUR

1 TEASPOON BAKING POWDER

1/2 TEASPOON SALT

1 EGG

1. Turn the oven on to 375° F and make sure the rack is in the middle of the oven. With a little soft butter, grease the inside of an 8-inch square baking dish (or a 9- or 10-inch round baking dish).

2. Peel the apples with a paring knife. Hold the apple in one hand and the knife in your other hand. Start at the top and

EQUIPMENT LIST

8-INCH SQUARE BAKING DISH
  OR A 9- OR 10-INCH ROUND
  BAKING DISH

PARING KNIFE OR 8-INCH
  SERRATED KNIFE

CUTTING BOARD

LARGE BOWL

MEASURING CUPS

MEASURING SPOONS

2 SMALL BOWLS

SMALL SAUCEPAN

LARGE SPOON

FORK

BAKING SHEET

ALUMINUM FOIL

KITCHEN TIMER

POT HOLDERS

turn the apple around and around as you peel, cutting away the skin in a spiral. Be patient. You will get better with every apple you peel.

3. One at a time, put the apples on a cutting board, stem end up. Holding the apple carefully with one hand, cut down through the middle of the apple, slicing it in half. Put each half cut side down on the board. From the outer side, start cutting thin slices the thickness of a cracker, and move toward the core in the center. Then turn the piece around and do the same from the other side. Finally flip the piece over and slice off the last pieces from the core. Discard the core, and put the apple slices in a large bowl.

4. Combine 1/2 cup of the sugar and 2 tablespoons flour in a small bowl and stir well. Sprinkle the mixture over the apples and toss with your hands to mix. Put the apples in the buttered baking dish and set aside.

5. To make the crisp topping, melt the stick of butter in a small pan over low heat. Watch it so it doesn't burn. When it has melted, set it aside.

VARIATIONS

You can also make this crisp with peaches or pears. Just use 6 cups sliced peaches or pears instead of apples. (You will need about 8 large ripe peaches or from 6 to 8 ripe pears.) Peel the fruit. If you're using peaches, cut thin slices away from the pit and throw the pit away. If you're using pears, cut them in half and cut thin slices away from the core the same way you prepared the apples.

6. Put 1 cup flour, the remaining 3/4 cup sugar, 1 teaspoon baking powder, and 1/2 teaspoon salt in the bowl you first had the apples in. Stir everything with a large spoon until well mixed.

7. Crack the egg into a small bowl. Stir briskly with a fork until yolk and white are blended together and the egg is all yellow.

8. Pour the egg into the flour mixture and stir with a fork or rub the flour and egg between your fingers to make the mixture crumbly.

9. Sprinkle the crumbly topping evenly over the fruit, using your fingers to spread it out to the edges of the dish. With a large spoon, dribble the melted butter evenly over the topping. Try your best to cover all the crumbs with butter.

10. Set a baking sheet covered with aluminum foil on the middle rack of the oven. Put the dish on the baking sheet. The foil will catch any dripping juices. Set the timer for 30 minutes, and when the timer goes off, remove the baking dish with pot holders and check the dessert. See if the top of the crisp is a deep golden color. Also, poke a knife down in the center to make sure the apples are soft. If it isn't ready, set the timer for 10 more minutes. This crisp usually takes about 40 minutes. Serve warm with whipped cream or vanilla ice cream. When you dish it up, use a large spoon to scoop a portion onto each plate and be sure to serve some of the topping with every portion.

APPLE PIE

When I was growing up almost everyone would serve a slice of yellow cheddar cheese with warm apple pie, but nowadays most people prefer a scoop of vanilla ice cream alongside their warm pie. The ice cream is perfect when it is just starting to melt; it is like a cold, creamy sauce.

5 LARGE FIRM APPLES

2/3 CUP SUGAR

1/2 TEASPOON GROUND CINNAMON

FOR THE PIE DOUGH:

    2 CUPS ALL-PURPOSE FLOUR, PLUS A LITTLE

        MORE FOR DUSTING THE BOARD

    1/2 TEASPOON SALT

    2/3 CUP VEGETABLE SHORTENING

    1/2 CUP COLD WATER

TO GO WITH THE APPLE PIE:

    VANILLA ICE CREAM

EQUIPMENT LIST

PARING KNIFE OR 8-INCH
    SERRATED KNIFE

CUTTING BOARD

LARGE BOWL

MEASURING CUPS

MEASURING SPOONS

SMALL BOWL

LARGE MIXING BOWL

FORK

8-INCH PIE PAN

ROLLING PIN

METAL SPATULA

KITCHEN SCISSORS

BAKING SHEET

ALUMINUM FOIL

KITCHEN TIMER

POT HOLDERS

COOLING RACK

PREPARING THE APPLES:

1. Peel the apples and cut them in half. Lay each half cut side down on a cutting board, and cut thin slices (see page 137). Discard the core and put the apple slices in a large bowl.

2. Put the 2/3 cup sugar and 1/2 teaspoon cinnamon in a small bowl. Stir until they are mixed together and look light brown. Sprinkle the cinnamon sugar over the apple slices. Toss the slices with your hands until they are coated with the cinnamon sugar. Set aside.

MAKING THE PIE DOUGH:

3. Turn the oven on to 425° F. Make sure the oven rack is in the middle.

4. Put 2 cups flour and 1/2 teaspoon salt into a large mixing bowl. Stir the flour and salt together.

5. Fill a 1/3 cup measure with shortening. Scoop the shortening out of the cup with your fingers and put it in the bowl with the flour. Do this one more time so you have 2/3 cup shortening in the bowl.

6. Flour your hands, then roll the shortening around in the flour so it isn't too sticky to handle. Break the shortening into 4 or 5 smaller pieces and coat them all with flour in the bowl. Then lightly rub the shortening and flour together with your fingers for about a minute to make little lumps. If there is loose flour on the bottom of the bowl, scoop it up to the top with your fingers and rub shortening into it to make more lumps. Work lightly, letting the bits of shortening and flour fall back into the bowl. When most of the flour and shortening has been transformed into lots of little lumps and the mixture looks like grated cheese, you have mixed enough.

7. Sprinkle the cold water over the dough. Stir the dough with a fork until the water disappears.

8. Reach down into the very bottom of the bowl and gather up all the pieces of the dough. Now pat and press the dough together until you have a ball of dough.

9. Sprinkle a large cutting board or a countertop lightly with a small handful of flour. Spread the flour into a circle bigger than your 8-inch pie pan.

10. Put the dough in the center of the circle of flour and pull it apart into two equal pieces. Gently press one half into a rough ball. Put it on the floured board or counter.

Flour the rolling part of a rolling pin. Flatten the dough a little with the rolling pin, then begin rolling from the center of the dough out to the edges to make a circle. Don't roll back and forth. Move the dough now and then to make sure it isn't sticking to the surface. If it is, slide a metal spatula in a wiggling motion under the dough to loosen it, sprinkle more flour on the board underneath it, then continue to roll out the dough into a big circle. It should be about as thin as a cracker and about 1 1/2 inches larger all around than your pie pan. Put the pie pan upside down in the center of the dough to measure it.

11. Gently slide a metal spatula under the dough to lift it off the surface. Fold the dough in half. Put the dough into the pie pan, with the fold in the center of the pan. Now unfold the dough so it covers and hangs over the edge of the pie pan. Gently press the dough against the inside of the pie pan. In places where there is more than about an inch of dough hanging over the edge, trim it way with scissors or a knife.

12. Lightly dust the board or counter again with a little more flour and put down the other half of the dough. Roll out another circle as you did the first one. Fold it in half.

13. Pile the apple slices into the dough-lined pie pan. It should be full and a little mounded in the center. Press the apples down gently with your hands.

14. With a spatula, lift the folded dough from the board and place it on top of the pie, with the fold in the middle. Unfold the dough to cover all the apples.

15. If there is more than about an inch of dough hanging over the edge, trim the extra dough away. Press together the top dough and the bottom dough around the edge of the pie pan, tucking the overhanging dough under itself all the way around. Be sure to keep all the dough on top of the rim. Now, using a finger of one hand to hold the rim of the dough in place, making sure that it doesn't slip over under the rim, with your other hand press the prongs of a fork down on the edge of the dough all the way around the pie. This seals the edges together and makes a neat design. Make a few small slits with a knife in the top crust so the steam will escape as the pie bakes.

Serving the complete chicken dinner on the terrace

A beautiful frosted birthday cake

16. Line a baking sheet with aluminum foil and set it on the middle rack of the oven. Put the pie on the foil-lined baking sheet. The foil will catch any bubbling, dripping juices.

17. Set the timer for 15 minutes. After 15 minutes, lower the oven temperature to 350° F, and reset the timer for 30 minutes. When the timer rings, use pot holders to remove the pie from the oven and set it on the stove top. Stick a fork through the top crust of the pie in the middle. If the fork can easily pierce the crust and the apples feel soft, the pie is done. The crust should also be lightly golden and there will probably be apple juices bubbling around the edges. If the pie is not done, return it to the oven and set the timer for 10 minutes and then check the pie again.

18. When the pie is done, use your pot holders to remove the pie from the oven and put it on a cool stove burner or on a rack. Serve and eat it warm, if you can, with vanilla ice cream.

Chapter 14

CHICKEN DINNER

1. **HOW TO MAKE A BREAD STUFFING WITH TOASTED BREAD.**

2. **HOW TO ROAST A CHICKEN.**

3. **HOW TO BRAISE VEGETABLES.**

4. **HOW TO MAKE A SIDE DISH (THE VEGETABLES) TOGETHER WITH THE MAIN DISH (THE CHICKEN AND STUFFING), SO THAT THE WHOLE MEAL IS READY TO BE SERVED AT THE SAME TIME.**

Making a whole meal for the first time is a little like climbing to the top of Mount Everest. It takes planning and practice. In this meal, the chicken and stuffing bake together in a roasting pan (or roast together in a baking dish, which is pretty much the same thing), and the vegetables will braise inside

a covered casserole dish. ("Brais-
ing" means cooking food slowly with a
little liquid in a covered container.) When
you sit down and start eating tender roast chicken, buttery sage stuffing,
and moist tasty carrots, potatoes, and onions, notice how delicious all these
flavors are together. Some things taste good together and some things don't.
Recognizing what things do is an important part of learning to cook a
whole meal.

I haven't included a recipe for dessert for this meal. You could make
a pie or a crisp, but the first time you are preparing a complete chicken
dinner, keep the rest of the meal simple. You might just have a dish of your
favorite ice cream.

ROAST CHICKEN, BREAD STUFFING, and BRAISED VEGETABLES

Usually when we stuff a chicken or a turkey for a special occasion like Sunday dinner or Thanksgiving, we spoon the stuffing into the cavity of a big bird. But here you are going to learn a much simpler way to make a stuffed roast chicken for an everyday dinner.

EQUIPMENT LIST

KITCHEN TIMER

TONGS OR A FORK

LARGE BOWL

PARING KNIFE OR 8-INCH
  SERRATED KNIFE

CUTTING BOARD

SMALL BOWL

MEDIUM-SIZED SKILLET

LARGE SPOON

MEASURING SPOONS

MEASURING CUPS

13- BY 9- BY 2-INCH BAKING
  PAN FOR THE CHICKEN

VEGETABLE PEELER

1- TO 1 1/2-QUART CASSEROLE
  DISH (WITH LID) FOR THE
  VEGETABLES

SMALL SAUCEPAN

POT HOLDERS

SAGE BREAD STUFFING:

8 SLICES WHITE BREAD

2 STALKS CELERY

1 SMALL ONION

4 TABLESPOONS BUTTER

1/2 TEASPOON SALT

1/4 TEASPOON BLACK PEPPER

1 1/2 TEASPOONS DRIED SAGE OR

  1 TABLESPOON CHOPPED FRESH SAGE

1/2 CUP CHICKEN BROTH OR WATER

148

ROAST CHICKEN:

2 1/2-POUND CHICKEN, SPLIT IN TWO

VEGETABLE SHORTENING FOR GREASING

THE PAN

SALT AND PEPPER

BRAISED VEGETABLES:

4 CARROTS

2 ONIONS

8 SMALL RED POTATOES

3 TABLESPOONS BUTTER

1/4 CUP WATER

SALT AND PEPPER

MAKING THE SAGE BREAD STUFFING:

1. Turn the oven on to 225° F. Spread the bread slices in a single layer on the oven rack, keeping them a little apart. Set the kitchen timer for 35 minutes. When the bell rings turn the slices over with tongs or a fork. Let the bread dry out 15 more minutes and then take a slice and break it in half. If it is still soft in the middle, put it back and let the bread dry out 15 more minutes. Dry bread has much better taste and texture than fresh bread when it is baked in a stuffing. When the bread is completely dry, take it out of the oven and put it in a large bowl. Use your hands to break up the bread into lots of little pieces.

2. Cut each of the 2 celery stalks lengthwise into 3 long pieces. Then cut these crosswise into small pieces. Put the chopped celery into a small bowl.

3. Trim off the stem end of the onion and the fuzzy little roots. Peel off the papery outside skin. Cut the onion in half from the top, stem end to the bottom, root end. Put the onion halves on a cutting board, cut side down. Cut each half crosswise into about 8 slices, and then cut the slices into thirds so you end up with lots of small pieces. Put the chopped onion into the bowl with the celery.

4. Set a medium-sized skillet on the stove burner and turn on the heat to medium-low. Put the 4 tablespoons butter into the skillet, and when it has melted a little, tilt the skillet—up, down, and around, so the that the melted butter covers the bottom. Add the chopped celery and onion to the skillet, and stir them around with a big spoon, spreading them evenly around the skillet. Cook and stir for about 3 minutes, until the onion has softened a little. Test to see if it has softened by taking a few pieces of onion out with the spoon, letting them cool a minute, and tasting to see if the onion has lost its crispness. If it hasn't, keep cooking and stirring and test again in 2 minutes. When the celery and onion have cooked, add them to the bowl of bread pieces.

Add the 1/2 teaspoon salt, 1/4 teaspoon pepper, and the dried 1 1/2 teaspoons or 1 tablespoon fresh sage. If you're using dried sage, taste a little pinch of it, and if it doesn't have much flavor, add an extra teaspoon. Mix the stuffing with your hands, reaching to the bottom of the bowl and tossing, so all the flavors mingle with the bread.

5. Drizzle the 1/2 cup broth or water over the stuffing. Toss and mix the stuffing lightly with your hands again, until all the ingredients are moist and well mixed. The stuffing should not be wet, just softened and damp. Taste and add a little more salt, pepper, or sage, if needed.

THE HERB SAGE:
A GIFT OF FLAVOR IN BREAD STUFFING

How would it feel to live in a world where everyone was wise and lived forever? During the Middle Ages, many people believed that if you ate sage leaves, you would become very wise and live for many, many years. We know today this isn't true.

Sage was also used as a medicine by the Greeks and Romans, thousands of years ago, and by Native Americans, who mixed sage leaves with bear grease to heal sores and to treat snake bites. The Chinese thought sage leaves made one of the finest teas.

The wild plant called sagebrush that grows in the high desert is not the same plant as the sage that we use in cooking. It smells good, but it tastes very unpleasant. You can plant the sage for cooking in your own backyard. Sometimes you can find fresh sage leaves for sale at a farmers' market or at the supermarket, and you can always buy it dried. The sage we grow has a strong, sharp, rather bitter, but pleasing taste. It is hard to describe because it has a flavor all its own. For our stuffing we can use either dried sage, crumbled or ground up, or finely chopped fresh leaves.

PREPARING THE CHICKEN:

6. Turn the oven on to 425° F. Make sure the oven rack is in the middle of the oven. Wash the chicken halves under cold running water. Pat them dry with paper towels.

7. You need a baking pan or an ovenproof baking dish large enough for the 2 chicken halves to sit side by side without crowding. Grease the pan with a little vegetable shortening.

8. Divide the stuffing in half. Make 2 rounded mounds of stuffing at either end of the baking dish. Salt and pepper the skin of each chicken half. Put each half on top of a mound of stuffing. Set aside while you prepare the vegetables.

PREPARING THE VEGETABLES:

9. Slice off the stem top and root tip of the 4 carrots. Hold each carrot by its thick top with one hand and with the other, hold a vegetable peeler. Slide the peeler down—from the top where you are holding the carrot to the bottom—digging in just enough to remove the peel. Turn the carrot and repeat until the whole carrot is peeled. Cut each carrot into 4 pieces and put them into an ovenproof casserole dish with a lid.

10. Trim, peel, and cut the 2 onions in half the way you did to the onion for the stuffing. Then cut each onion half in two crosswise, so you end up with 8 pieces of onion. Add the onions to the carrots in the casserole

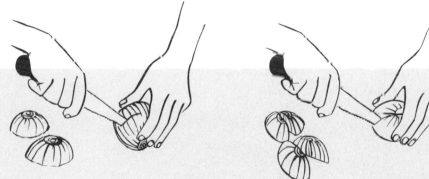

11. Wash the 8 small potatoes and dry with paper towels. Don't peel them. If they are larger than a golf ball, cut them in half. Add them to the casserole with the onions and carrots.

12. Put the 3 tablespoons butter and 1/4 cup water into a small saucepan and turn the heat on to medium. Stir while the butter melts and mixes with the water. As soon as the butter and water are blended, remove from the heat, and pour the liquid over the vegetables in the casserole. Lightly salt and pepper the vegetables. Stir the vegetables with a large spoon so every vegetable is coated with the butter and water mixture. Put the lid on the casserole.

13. Put the chicken and the vegetables in the oven at the same time. If you have to, place the vegetable casserole behind the chicken—but both should be on the middle rack. Set the timer for 45 minutes. When the bell rings, using pot holders, take the chicken dish from the oven and put it on the stove top. With the tip of a small paring knife, cut into a chicken leg at the joint between the drumstick and the thigh. If the juices are clear, the chicken is done. If the juices are pink or red, put the dish back into the oven and cook 15 minutes more.

14. When the chicken is done, carefully take the pan out of the oven with pot holders and put it on the stove top or another heat-proof surface. The stuffing around the edges of the chicken will be crisp and dark brown; the stuffing under the chicken will be moist and soft. Take out the vegetable dish with pot holders and put it nearby. With your serrated knife, cut each chicken half in two, cutting between the leg and the wing to make 4 portions. Dish up a portion of chicken, stuffing, and vegetables on each plate, and serve.

WHAT YOU NEED TO THINK ABOUT TO PLAN A MEAL

What foods look and taste good together? You want to try for a balance in both color and texture: something green and something light-colored, something crunchy and something soft. You don't have to be an artist. Just don't serve mashed potatoes, pancakes, and sliced white bread all together for a meal because all these things are pale, white, and soft in texture, and they will taste similar and dull together. A meal you would love to meet at the table would be: a slice of warm, juicy, browned meatloaf with a hot, buttery baked potato and a crisp, green salad. A chocolate brownie would make a perfect end to this supper.

Chapter 15

CUPCAKES and a BIRTHDAY CAKE

CUPCAKES and a BIRTHDAY CAKE

1. HOW TO MIX CAKE BATTERS.

2. HOW TO FILL INDIVIDUAL CUPCAKE CONTAINERS AND TOP THEM WITH A CRUMB MIX.

3. HOW TO PREPARE A CAKE PAN FOR FILLING.

4. HOW TO BAKE CAKES AND TEST FOR DONENESS.

5. HOW TO UNMOLD CAKES.

6. HOW TO MAKE A FROSTING.

7. HOW TO FROST A CAKE.

Jessica, one of my students, summed up how many of us feel about cupcakes when she said, "I wish cupcakes had little wings and could fly into my hand whenever I wanted one."

For a special birthday, instead of going to the store and looking for a present, make your friend a chocolate cake, complete with candles on the top. Everyone will like it more, because you made it.

BUTTERMILK CRUMB CUPCAKES

When my children were in elementary school I used to bake these cupcakes every year for the Bake Day Sale, to help raise money for the school. I baked so many cupcakes during those years that if they were put in a straight line I'll bet they would go from California to New York. They were the most popular item at the bake sale.

EQUIPMENT LIST

MUFFIN PAN

SMALL BOWL

FORK

MEASURING CUPS

MEASURING SPOONS

LARGE MIXING BOWL

LARGE SPOON

KITCHEN TIMER

POT HOLDERS

COOLING RACK

VEGETABLE SHORTENING FOR GREASING MUFFIN
    CUPS

1 EGG

1 1/4 CUPS FLOUR

1 CUP LIGHT-BROWN SUGAR (PUSH THE SUGAR
    FIRMLY DOWN INTO THE MEASURING CUP.)

1/4 TEASPOON SALT

1/3 CUP VEGETABLE SHORTENING

1 TEASPOON BAKING POWDER

1/4 TEASPOON BAKING SODA

1/4 TEASPOON GROUND CINNAMON

1/4 TEASPOON GROUND NUTMEG

1/2 CUP BUTTERMILK

1. Turn the oven on to 350° F. Grease the inside of 7 muffin pan cups with a little vegetable shortening, using your fingers.

2. Crack open the egg and drop it into a small bowl. Stir the egg briskly with a fork until the white and yolk are mixed together and the egg is all yellow.

3. Put the 1 1/4 cups flour, 1 cup brown sugar, and 1/4 teaspoon salt in a large mixing bowl. Stir with a fork to get it well mixed.

4. Add 1/3 cup vegetable shortening to the bowl with the flour and brown sugar.

5. Lightly rub the shortening and flour together with your fingertips, letting the bits fall back in the bowl. Keep reaching to the bottom and all around the sides of the bowl and rubbing the shortening and flour together to make crumbs. When the mixture looks like coarse bread crumbs, you have mixed enough. Remove 1/4 cup of this crumb mixture and set aside to sprinkle on top of the cupcakes just before they bake.

6. Add the 1 teaspoon baking powder, 1/4 teaspoon baking soda, 1/4 teaspoon cinnamon, and 1/4 teaspoon nutmeg to the flour mixture that remains in the bowl and stir it all around with a fork so it is mixed together. Add the 1/2 cup buttermilk and the beaten egg, and for the last time, stir everything together with a large spoon so the batter is mixed well.

7. Use a large spoon to put the batter into the greased cups of the muffin pan, filling each one about half full. Sprinkle the top of the batter in each cup with 1 rounded teaspoon of the crumb mixture you set aside. Put the muffin pan in the oven and set the timer for 15 minutes. When the timer rings, take a pot holder, pull the muffin pan toward you to the edge of the oven rack, and stick a toothpick in the center of one of the cupcakes. If the toothpick comes out clean with no gooey batter on it, the cupcakes are done. If there is batter sticking to the toothpick, push the muffin pan back into the oven, set the timer for 5 more minutes, and continue to bake the cupcakes. When the timer goes off again, check them again for doneness.

8. When the cupcakes are done, use pot holders to remove the muffin pan from the oven. Put it on a rack and let the cupcakes cool in the pan for 10 minutes. Then they will lift right out. If they're sticking a little, run a knife carefully around the edges of each one and then gently lift them out of the pan and put them on a plate.

CHOCOLATE
BIRTHDAY CAKE

MAKES ONE 8-INCH ROUND CAKE (OR ABOUT 9 CUPCAKES)

Once upon a time there were nine little cupcakes that felt very insignificant. More than anything in the world they wanted to become one big chocolate birthday cake. When you make this birthday cake you will make their dream come true.

If you want to be mean, you can make cupcakes instead of a cake with this recipe. Just set the timer for 15 minutes when you put them in the oven and test them when the bell rings—nine little cupcakes bake faster than one big cake.

You can serve this cake with just confectioners' sugar dusted on top but if it is for a special occasion like a birthday you will want to frost it.

VEGETABLE SHORTENING FOR GREASING THE PAN

1 TABLESPOON FLOUR FOR DUSTING THE PAN

5 TABLESPOONS BUTTER

1 1/2 CUPS FLOUR

1 CUP SUGAR

1/4 CUP UNSWEETENED COCOA

1 TEASPOON BAKING SODA

1/2 TEASPOON SALT

1 TABLESPOON CIDER VINEGAR

2 TEASPOONS VANILLA EXTRACT

1 CUP WATER

OPTIONAL: CONFECTIONERS' SUGAR FOR DUSTING
   THE CAKE

EQUIPMENT LIST

8-INCH ROUND CAKE PAN

MEASURING SPOONS

SMALL SAUCEPAN

MEASURING CUPS

LARGE MIXING BOWL

LARGE SPOON

SMALL BOWL

RUBBER SPATULA

KITCHEN TIMER

POT HOLDERS

COOLING RACK

KNIFE

LARGE PLATE

METAL SPATULA

1. Turn the oven on to 350° F. Make sure the rack is set in the middle.

2. Use your fingers to grease the bottom and sides of an 8-inch round cake pan with a little vegetable shortening. Sprinkle 1 tablespoon flour into the pan. Tilt the pan around, shaking it a little, until the bottom and sides are lightly covered with flour. Then turn the pan upside down over the sink or into the trash basket and tap the pan firmly so any extra flour falls out. Set the pan aside.

3. Put the 5 tablespoons butter in a small saucepan on the stove and turn the heat to low. Stand right by the stove and keep an eye on the butter. As soon as it has melted, set the pan aside and let the butter cool a little.

4. Put the 1 1/2 cups flour, 1 cup sugar, 1/4 cup cocoa, 1 teaspoon baking soda, and 1/2 teaspoon salt in a large mixing bowl. Stir with a large spoon until the ingredients are well mixed.

5. Pour the 1 tablespoon vinegar, 2 teaspoons vanilla, and 1 cup water into a small bowl and stir them until they are well mixed.

6. Add the liquid mixture into the flour mixture, and then stir in the melted butter. Now roll up your sleeves and with a big spoon in one hand, holding onto the bowl firmly with your other, stir the batter fiercely for about a minute until it looks very thick, smooth, and creamy.

7. Pour the batter into the cake pan, and use a rubber spatula to get it all out of the bowl. Then gently spread it evenly in the pan.

8. Put the pan in the oven and set the timer for 25 minutes. When the timer bell goes off, use a pot holder to pull the cake out enough so you can test it for doneness by sticking a toothpick into the center. If the toothpick comes out clean, the cake is done. If the toothpick has some sticky batter on it when you remove it, let the cake bake another 5 to 10 minutes. This cake usually takes about 30 minutes to bake.

9. Remove the cake from the oven with pot holders. Set it on a rack, and let it cool 10 minutes.

10. Turn the cake upside down onto a large plate. If the cake doesn't come right out of the pan, loosen it by running a knife carefully around the sides, between the cake and the pan, and then carefully push a metal spatula under the bottom of the cake to loosen it. This cake, however, usually comes right out of the pan without coaxing.

11. When cool, the cake can be dusted with confectioners' sugar and served. For a special occasion, be grand and make the Portsmouth Frosting that follows and decorate your cake with it.

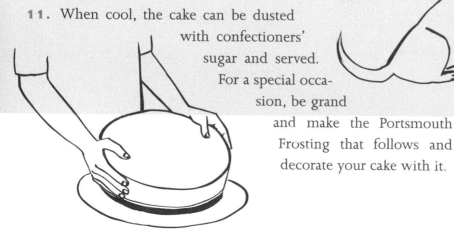

PORTSMOUTH FROSTING

MAKES ABOUT 1 1/2 CUPS FROSTING

This frosting recipe makes a little more than you will need to frost your cake, but it is better to have too much rather than not enough. Put any extra frosting in a little jar, screw on a lid, and store it in the refrigerator. It will keep almost forever, and it comes in handy for frosting graham crackers or cookies for a friend after school.

EQUIPMENT LIST

SMALL SAUCEPAN

MIXING BOWL

MEASURING CUPS

MEASURING SPOONS

LARGE SPOON

4 TABLESPOONS (1/2 STICK) BUTTER

1/4 CUP WHIPPING CREAM, PLUS A LITTLE MORE

    FOR THINNING OUT THE FROSTING IF IT IS TOO

    THICK AND STIFF TO SPREAD

2 TEASPOONS VANILLA EXTRACT

1/4 TEASPOON SALT

3 CUPS CONFECTIONERS' SUGAR (POWDERED

    SUGAR), PLUS MORE IF NECESSARY

1. Put the 4 tablespoons butter in a small saucepan on the stove and turn the heat to low. Stand right by the stove and watch it carefully. As soon as the butter has melted, pour it into a mixing bowl. Let it cool for 2 or 3 minutes.

2. Add the 1/4 cup cream and 2 teaspoons vanilla to the butter. Stir with a large spoon until it is well mixed.

3. Add the 1/4 teaspoon salt and 1 1/2 cups of the confectioners' sugar to the butter mixture and stir until it is creamy and smooth. Add another 1 1/2 cups confectioners' sugar to the frosting and keep stirring until it is smooth and spreadable. You want the frosting to be like peanut butter—creamy, but not runny. If it's thicker than you want, add a little cream, only 1 tablespoon at a time; it shouldn't need much more than just 1 tablespoon. If it's too thin, gradually add 1/2 cup more confectioners' sugar. If it's still too thin, add more, but only 1/4 cup at a time, stirring hard all around the bottom and sides of the bowl.

FROSTING YOUR CAKE:
Decorating a cake with a thick creamy frosting is a little like spreading peanut butter on a slice of bread. Use a long, thin spatula or knife. Scoop up some frosting and spread it on the sides of the cake first. Work carefully, turning the plate around until you have frosted all the sides. Use your spatula or knife to smooth the sides. Then scoop up more frosting and spread it evenly over the top. The cake doesn't have to look perfect, so don't get too fussy about a dent or a mark! A homemade cake is supposed to look as though someone made it, not like a factory cake. You can finish the cake by putting candles on it, if it's for a birthday.

Index

Pies
    apple, 134, 135, 139–45
    dough for, 134, 135,
        140–44
Pizza, 116–19
    dough for, 109–15
Popovers, 54–55, 61–63
Portsmouth frosting, 164–65
Potatoes
    baked, 80–81
    braised with carrots and
        onions, 149, 153–55
    vegetable soup with, 3, 6
Potholders, 26
Pyrex cups, 61, 63

Raisins, chewy oatmeal
    cookies with, 128–30
Red leaf lettuce, 14
Rice, 28–37
    baked, 32–33
    boiled, 30–31
    importance of, 3
    varieties, 29
    vegetable soup with, 3, 6
    vegetable stir-fry with,
        34–37
Romaine lettuce, 14
Russet potatoes, 80

Safety, xiii
Sage, 82, 151
    bread stuffing with,
        148–51
Salad, 10–19
    chicken, 19
    green, 14–15
    ham, 19
    tuna, 16–19
    turkey, 19
Salad dressing
    oil and vinegar, 12–13
    for tuna salad, 19
Salsa, baked potatoes with, 80
Saucepans, how to measure, 7
Sauces
    cream, 93, 104
    summer tomato, 93–96
    winter tomato, 93, 97–98
Scallions
    in summer tomato sauce,
        94–96
    in vegetable stir-fry, 36
Scissors, cutting herbs with,
    85
Scraps, saving, 33
Serrated knives, 9
Shortcake, 72–74
    strawberry, 75–77
Shortening, 68
Skillets, measuring, 41
Slicing, tools for, 9
Slotted spoons, 31

Soup, vegetable, 2–9
Sour cream, omelet with
    avocado and, 52–53
Spaghetti, 99–100
    with summer tomato
        sauce, 94–96
Spatulas, 24
    for frosting, 165
Spoons
    ladles, 8
    long-handled, 33
    measuring, 56
    slotted, 31
Steak, supper, 120–25
Stir-frying, 29, 34–37
Stove, learning to use, 8
Strainers, 14, 31, 101, 106
Strawberry shortcake, 75–77
Stuffing, bread, 146–55
Sugar, measuring, 56

Tablespoons, 56
Teaspoons, 56
Thyme, 82, 91
    in herb butter for sautéed
        zucchini, 89–91
Tomatoes
    baked potato with, 80
    pizza with, 116–19
    preparing, 6

A Note About the Author

Marion Cunningham was born in southern California and now lives in Walnut Creek, near San Francisco. She was responsible for the complete revision of *The Fannie Farmer Cookbook* and is the author of *The Fannie Farmer Baking Book*, *The Breakfast Book*, and *The Supper Book*. She travels frequently throughout the country giving cooking demonstrations, has contributed articles to *Bon Appétit*, *Food & Wine*, and *Gourmet* magazines, and writes a column for the San Francisco *Chronicle* and the Los Angeles *Times*. For the past two years she has been giving cooking classes for children.

A Note on the Type

The text of this book was set in Monotype Joanna, a typeface designed by Eric Gill, the noted English stonecutter, typographer, and illustrator. It was released by the Monotype Corporation in 1937. Reflecting Eric Gill's idiosyncratic approach to type design, Joanna has a number of playful features, chief among them the design of the italic companion as a narrow sloped roman.

Composed by North Market Street Graphics,
Lancaster, Pennsylvania
Printed and bound by Rand McNally Book Services,
Taunton, Massachusetts
Designed by Barbara de Wilde
Layouts by Wendy Byrne